A FUTURE FOR
THE FREE CHURCHES?

CHRISTOPHER DRIVER

SCM PRESS LTD
BLOOMSBURY STREET LONDON

For
R.W.C., D.T.J., E.R.R., D.G.S.
Ministers of my faith
and order

First published 1962
© SCM Press Ltd 1962
Printed by Charles Birchall & Sons, Ltd.,
Liverpool & London

THE LIVING CHURCH BOOKS

Christianity today is confronted by such challenges that all Christians need to be well informed about the truths, strengths and enjoyments which are theirs in their heritage. They need to know, too, about the many experiments and reassessments which are renewing the Church for its mission in the contemporary world. Our aim in the Living Church Books is to contribute to the intensive educational effort which the crisis demands.

CONTENTS

ACKNOWLEDGEMENTS

For the germ of this book, and for a running commentary on its growth, I am deeply indebted to the Revd. Daniel Jenkins. Several other friends have read the manuscript in whole or in part, and I am particularly grateful for the detailed comments of the Revd. Kenneth Slack. The responsibility for what is printed naturally remains mine. Finally, for different kinds of forbearance, I would thank my wife, children, and publisher.

C.P.D.

INTRODUCTION

It is apparent that God is about a great worke, yea, to make a great change in the world, except we doe as it were hold his hand by seeking and turning unto him, and by removing the things that provoke him : he doth not lay all these stones, and move all these wheeles for nothing, and yet who knowes what it is he is about, till it bee brought forth? . . . There are certaine times and seasons wherein God troubleth the Churches, and that very thing that distinguishes between Nations and Churches, to be saved or to be destroyed, is the very ability to discerne of those seasons.—John Preston, *A Sensible Demonstration of the Deitie,* a sermon preached in 1627.

THIS book is written out of the conviction that 'there are certaine times and seasons wherein God troubleth the Churches', and that the tercentenary of the Great Ejectment, which many Christians in Britain have been celebrating in 1962, is just such a season. Consequently, what follows is intended for the most part as an essay in Dissenting self-criticism, rather than as Dissenting apologetic (of which we have inevitably had an earful in recent months). For this purpose, I have tried to write as though from the outside, looking in. The more successful I am, the more offensive my descriptions and judgements are likely to be, for if there is one generalization that one may confidently make about all branches of the Christian Church in this country, it is that they do not take kindly to the would-be helpful comments of outside observers. Readers will recall, for example, the mauling Mr Paul Ferris received for his (admittedly vulnerable) *Observer* articles on the clergy in 1960. I am quite happy to be mauled, but I should prefer criticism to be directed to what I say, rather than to my temerity in saying it. Let it be clear then from the start that I write from within the family, with involved detachment, affectionate disrespect.

Asked why I am a Christian, and among Christians a Dissenter, I should be tempted to reply 'because I was born one'. If my interlocutor were a Roman Catholic, I suppose he would be quite satisfied with this answer. If he were an agnostic, he would be puzzled by my apparently uncritical attitude to infantile influences. But if he were a Dissenter himself, he would probably be shocked. For among Dissenters, even among those who do not demand a datable spiritual crisis, a 'conversion experience', as a prerequisite for anyone claiming to be a Christian, churchmanship is conceived almost exclusively as a deliberate, conscious response by adult or adolescent to the personal call of Christ.

It is far from my intention to belittle this viewpoint: indeed, I largely subscribe to it. The thread of 'by faith alone', which runs from St Paul through Luther to the last paragraph of most sermons in most chapels on most Sunday evenings, has possessed incalculable force in the history and emotions of the Free Churches. Dissent, like any other national institution, has its epic heroes, and ours are men like Bunyan, Fox, Carey: men who laid themselves open to the Spirit of God and therefore became able to step outside the social and ecclesiastical environment into which they were born. By faith, we tell each other, they saw through and beyond their time, and acted out the new understanding which was given them. These heroes are part of a myth— in the true and religious sense of that word—without which the Free Churches would die at the roots and shrivel. Anglicans who cannot sense this, however sympathetic they are to Dissenting theology and devotion, miss the heart of the matter, and are rarely able to enjoy profitable conversation with Free Churchmen.

But this is by no means the whole truth about the Free Churches, and it was to emphasize this neglected aspect that I spoke of having been 'born into' Dissent. The Free Churches are not simply an aggregation of people who have found a conscious personal faith. They are an environment in their own right, possessing their own social climate and exerting their own pull on those who have a rich complex of memories bound up with them. If I try to imagine myself as a recent convert to Christianity, after a totally secular upbringing, I cannot think it probable that I would have *chosen* to be a Congregationalist (or a Baptist, or a Methodist, or a Quaker). Fifty years ago one might have felt differently, but today, except in a few localities, it is not a vital and enticing 'image' which these communions present to the casual passer-by and the interested inquirer.

I am therefore thrown back on other, less assertive ways of accounting for the Free Churchmanship which I now consciously own, and I realize that I am a Dissenter because I was brought up in a Dissenting ambience. I came to value this particular form of the Christian Way because I saw it lived, and because no effort was ever made to conceal from me its incidental inadequacies and absurdities. If in the ensuing pages I make much of Dissent's virtues and vices as a cultural as well as a purely religious force in this country's history, it is because I myself have felt this force. In human terms, I suppose myself to be a Christian because I had the providential good fortune to be born of Christian parents, and to be exposed at formative periods of my adolescence to the ministry of men whose minds and personalities and conception of the Gospel, expressed in their preaching, writing and conversation, spoke to that which the Spirit of God had implanted within me. But believer or not, I would still have been in some sense, even though a greatly diminished sense, a Dissenter.

But what have I dissented from? In a way, I am reluctant to answer this question, because it is a false one, resting on the negative which is implied in the word 'Dissent' but which is less clearly present in the reality for which 'Dissent' stands. Properly understood, the forms of churchmanship and the outlook on life whose safety was secured by the sacrifice of 1662 are concerned with assertions, not denials. In this book

I am primarily concerned with re-interpreting these assertions. I am trying, as many others in other traditions are
trying, to find how in the world as we have it today Christians can live collectively by grace under authority, steering
a true course between the Scylla of legalism and the
Charybdis of sentimentality. In this context, I am cautious
of defining what I am dissenting from.

Anglicanism? Hardly. I have dissented quite vigorously
from Anglicanism in some of its forms. From its calm
assumption of social and ecclesiastical superiority, from the
superstition of its fringe parties—both Anglo-Catholic and
Evangelical—from church parade, private baptism and public
school religion, good Lord, deliver us. But none of this is
Anglicanism as it is understood by the Anglicans I know
best. Had I been born into an Anglican family, I hope
I would have remained a slightly discontented but funda-
mentally convinced Anglican, as I am now—on the same
terms—a Free Churchman.

I quote, for I cannot resist it, the paean to Anglicanism
sung by the convinced Dissenter, Bernard Manning:

> No man, by taking thought, can become an Anglican.
> Anglicans, like poets, are born, not made. Genuine
> Anglicanism is one of the very finest things that this
> country has produced or can produce; I yield to no one
> in my affectionate appreciation of it; but it is like an
> English village or the Oxford manner or a sincere liking
> for roast beef and plum pudding. It is a growth of ages.
> More than one generation must contribute to it. Its essence
> is too subtle and delicate to be produced at will. The strong
> and beautiful and Christian part of Anglicanism is its un-
> conscious part. As soon as it becomes self-conscious it be-
> comes strident and unbeautiful. The man who chooses to
> be an Anglican is by definition no Anglican. The Anglican
> does not choose: he occurs.[1]

[1] 'Some Lapsed Dissenters' in *Congregational Quarterly*, April
1951.

This could only have been written by someone who knew that a man's religion is a rich, complex and all-embracing phenomenon, not solely to be interpreted in terms of creeds and church order. Moreover, underneath the affectionate irony, it makes a serious point. The tenor of the mildly scurrilous paper in which this passage occurs is that people should normally remain in that station of churchmanship to which it has pleased God to call them. This view is not altogether fashionable, but there is much to be said for it. I have much sympathy—more sympathy, I fancy, than Manning had—with those Dissenters, very many in recent generations, who have found that to remain in any mean-ingful sense Christian at all they have to abandon the church order in which they were brought up. If in my own late 'teens my knowledge and experience of Congregationalism had been limited to the particular church of which I was at the time a member, I could hardly have failed while at Oxford to rise to the lure of *Ecclesia Anglicana* dressed to kill. I am now very glad to have found out in time that my own ecclesiastical tradition could indeed exemplify the fellowship of the Holy Spirit, and offer a liturgical variety, an unself-conscious catholicity, an intellectual zest and an appetite for excellence not easily matched elsewhere.

A certain amount has been written lately about the peculiar problems faced by graduates, and especially graduate Dissenters, when they return to their local churches. I return to this topic in a subsequent chapter. But at the risk of con-tradicting myself later, it is here relevant to say this. It may indeed sometimes be depressing for a graduate or anyone else to return from a place where he has been able to share in the best gifts of his own and other confessional traditions, into a local chapel where

> the best lack all conviction, and the worst
> Are full of a passionate intensity

This is a more common experience than denominational pundits are normally ready to allow. But the depression, unless in exceptional circumstances, need not be permanent or ruinous. It has many more creative possibilities than the sense of futility which sits half-perceived on many chapelgoers—and not a few of their ministers—who reach and pass their prime of life without ever realizing in corporate church order their individual visions of the Christian life. Unless one is convinced from experience and not just from exhortation that the ore of one's own confessional tradition possesses some latent metal which, once extracted, the Great Church would value highly, responsible churchmanship in the present ecumenical thaw becomes impossible, and all that one can honestly do is seek sustenance where one can find it.

This process of church-tasting, greatly assisted by the social mobility of the times, is nowadays taking effect on the grand scale. There is a General Post between denominations, and the Free Churches are in some places gainers as well as losers. (I believe, for instance, that about a fifth of the membership of Carrs Lane Chapel in Birmingham is Anglican by upbringing.) No doubt this crumbling of the old sectarian tariff walls is to be applauded by ecumenists: personally, I can only muster two cheers for it. The General Post could continue for generations without the denominations concerned moving an inch nearer reunion, simply because each transfer of membership makes the comparative study of church orders and confessional cultures seem a specialized and irrelevant activity. I do not think it is. An instructed Christian ought, I am sure, to think many times before detaching himself from the context of his fathers' religious experience and attaching himself to a different set of Christian values and observances, even if he has persuaded himself that the new set is in some ways intrinsically superior. I am not a Dissenter because I think that Congregationalism or Methodism or Presbyterianism make it easier for individuals and societies to be recognizably Christian than do

Anglicanism or Roman Catholicism at their best. This position I believe to be untenable. I am a Dissenter because I learnt the faith in one particular corner of the Free Churches, because I value the people—both living and centuries dead—from whom I learnt it, and because I regard my own church order like all church orders as an adequate basic framework for the exercise of the Christian life, but needing laborious days of reformation from within before it can be taken up into the richness and variety of the future whole.

There is a small point of terminology which had better be cleared up from the start, and this is the shades of meaning which are to be given to such different terms as 'Dissent', 'Nonconformity' and 'the Free Churches'. The situation here is confused,[1] and any decision about the use of these terms has an element of the arbitrary. I believe my own usage can be defended on historical and theological grounds, but I adopt it primarily because it saves me from clumsy circumlocutions.

By the 'Free Churches' of my title I normally mean those communions whose names strike a faint spark of recognition in most English people: Baptists, Congregationalists, Methodists and Presbyterians. Much of my argument might embrace without difficulty such smaller bodies as the Moravians and the Churches of Christ, but I have no firsthand knowledge here, and had better not pretend to it. In some contexts the category might be extended to the Presbyterian Church of Scotland, which is not exactly Free, and in other contexts to the Society of Friends and the Salvation Army, which are not exactly Churches, but I leave this decision to the reader. In various cultural and historical connections 'the Free Churches' must also include the Unitarians—especially

[1] I refer the reader to Dr Erik Routley's discussion in *English Religious Dissent* (Cambridge 1961) pp. 7–9.

when one is writing from a Manchester address—but in the greater part of this book I assume that I am talking of people who worship the Triune God. Where I unambiguously intend to include the Unitarians I use 'Nonconformists' as a general descriptive term which is, however, too heavily loaded with Victorian overtones to serve my main purpose.

'Dissent' I use as a variant for 'the Free Churches', but it is a much older term, and should perhaps be distinguished. The Free Churches are the contemporary ecclesiastical institutions: Dissent is more than that, for it takes in the history and culture which has grown up round these institutions since 1662. And since it is occasionally necessary to distinguish Methodism, which is Dissent by culture rather than churchmanship, from Baptists, Congregationalists and Presbyterians, I use 'Orthodox Dissent' collectively for these last.

'Puritanism' has a chapter to itself.

Didsbury
May 1962

I

ARE THE FREE CHURCHES FREE?

> . . . the nonsense, the melancholy, the madness of the tabernacle.
> Sydney Smith.

ARE the Free Churches free? I believe that they are not, except in a comparatively unimportant sense, and that this notion of our freedom is one of our most crippling delusions. It is a great thing to be free, but it is easier to boast of than to achieve. The delusion of freedom commonly accompanies the delusion of power, as will be obvious to anyone who has noticed the kind of people who use the slogan 'Britain strong and free', and the occasions to which they apply it. Just as a country which has escaped the worst forms of political slavery tries to conceal from itself that it is at the mercy of forces, events and nations to which it can no longer dictate, so a religio-political movement like Dissent, which was rescued by its founding fathers from the ecclesiastical totalitarians, tries to convince itself that the inaugural breakthrough to freedom can somehow, given just a little extra spurt of energy, be repeated; that despite all the ways in which history has moulded and smoothed the Free Churches in the last three hundred years, any new Reformation needed must inevitably be initiated by them. Imagining themselves to be free, Dissenters have become the prisoners of their own history and sociology, on parole not to carry their protest against the established order far enough to disturb it.

The Real Situation

There are several possible ways of describing what has

happened. One rather brutal way is the use of statistics and casual observation. According to at least one responsible and sympathetic sociologist, the English Free Churches have lost about half their congregations in a half century during which the population of the country has risen by more than a half.[1] Numerically, the Anglicans have suffered hardly less severely. But each new census reveals a further trek away from the areas traditionally associated with 'the Nonconformist way of life', and additional statistics about the sociological composition of those who remain in chapel pews reveal a prospect far bleaker than one would gather from the whistling in the dark heard at the annual denominational assemblies, and the tentative treatment of the redundant chapel problem.

Nor do numbers reveal the worst of it. To visit those parts of the country where the chapels are most deeply embedded in the landscape and the local history, to live in Methodist Yorkshire or Baptist Wales or Independent East Anglia or Unitarian Lancashire, is to recognize the real plight of Nonconformity in the sixties. Anyone can point to shining exceptions in particular places, but over large tracts of country it is true that behind the peeling facades and the plaintive wayside pulpits there is nothing left but a faithful, ingrown

---

[1] Cf. Rowntree and Lavers, *English Life and Leisure* (Longmans, 1951), pp. 342–4. The following figures are given for church attendances in York on typical Sundays in 1901 and 1948.

	1901 (Adult pop. 48,000)	1948 (Adult pop. 78,500)
Anglicans	7,453	3,384
Free Churches	6,447	3,514
Roman Catholics	2,360	3,073

In the 1948 Free Church attendances, the proportion of males over 17 was 39 p.c. (then 47.6 p.c. in the population as a whole), and the proportion of over-fifties was 45.1 p.c. (35.4 p.c. in the population as a whole).

remnant, whiling away its Pleasant Sunday Afternoons and its Women's Bright Hours in dingy rooms from which whole generations and classes and intelligence levels have long since fled.

Looking at the Zephyrs, Minxes and Gazelles parked outside the more prosperous chapels of Mill Hill and Bournemouth and Ealing and Purley, it might seem premature to contemplate the obituary of the species, to start wondering, with Philip Larkin,

> When churches fall completely out of use
> What we shall turn them into . . .

And indeed, there are some localities, most conspicuously among the middle-class suburbs of large cities, where Free Churches are imitating the best features of their booming American counterparts, and developing as the neighbourly, civilizing religious institutions which are needed by the socially fluid districts in which they are set. There are a dozen good reasons for welcoming this development, and these churches at least afford a springboard rather than a quicksand from which to contemplate the future of Dissent. They have a great responsibility, and some of them are aware of it. But they are not in themselves a quick and easy answer to our problems, nor can they do very much to arrest the process which has pushed Dissent further and further towards the margin of English life, until it is nearly off the page altogether.

Dissent did not occupy the place it once did in English society simply because a few like-minded Christians with similar incomes banded together in each place to form chapels, subsequently realizing that they had discovered a good social coagulant. Both in their religious and in their social functions (and it is debatable whether the two can finally be separated) chapels were for centuries the natural self-expression of a substantial part of the entire English people. There were—and are—considerable regional variations in the strength of the Free Churches collectively, and of different denominations individually.[1] Scratch a Cornishman and you find a Methodist; scratch a Merseysider and you might perhaps find a Presbyterian. There is all the difference in the world between the English Presbyterian culture heavily influenced by educated expatriate Scots; and the Methodist culture, which was formed by deprived rural and industrial proletariats, raising themselves into the bourgeoisie by the grace of God and their own bootstraps. But both cultures put down deep roots, as did the even older Puritan culture to which I return in the next chapter. Any rescue operation on the Free Churches which forgets this is doomed to failure, and any idea that the pullulating chapels of suburb and housing estate can easily find themselves a comparable niche in the national mind is an illusion. A niche may be found, but it will be a very different one.

How then has it come to pass that the Free Churches today stand for little in the public mind but bad architecture and good works, both presented with an air of lingering, no longer quite convinced, disapproval? It is not only 'the public' which sees this as a just criticism. Envisaging, thirty years ago, the upbringing of a typical (though of course imaginary) 'lapsed Dissenter', Bernard Manning wrote: 'Nonconformity as it was presented to and embraced by him was a sturdy, severe, somewhat crude affair, morally bracing, but aesthetically weak, and intellectually nondescript.'[2]

This may not have been my experience, or yours. But English churches, like English public schools or restaurants, can expect to be judged by what is normal rather than by what is best. Stick a pin into the Free Church year-books; choose at random half a dozen chapels up and down the

[1] Cf. Tillyard, 'The Distribution of the Free Churches in England', *Sociological Review* Vol. XXVII (1935) Cited in Payne, *The Free Church Tradition in the Life of England* (SCM Press, 1944), p. 170.
[2] *Op. cit.*

country; attend their services; talk to their ministers, members and adherents; and the general justice of the description can hardly fail to strike you, even though you may be made aware, here and there, of qualities in the life of the chapels whose existence you had not previously suspected.

Perhaps part of the trouble is that the Free Churches have never been much disturbed by what the public thinks of them. For centuries they were obliged to assert their convictions against general revilement, from High Tory vicars and low life rakes, London wits and Birmingham roughs. A sizeable book was recently published which was devoted entirely to the satirists' assaults on early Methodism.[1] 'At all times, in all places, and in all persons,' wrote Manning, 'English Dissent has an unfailing characteristic: *quod semper, quod ubique, et quod ab omnibus*—it is the test of Dissent as well as catholicity—and the unfailing characteristic of Dissent is this: *it is not done.*' The corollary of this is that in the folklore of the Free Churches, the public is always wrong. It is perhaps time that this comfortable assumption was questioned. Certainly, the public's opinion of a Christian church is not to be accepted without reserve. 'Blessed are ye when all men shall revile you and persecute you.' But it is doubtful whether this saying is entirely applicable to the Church in contemporary Britain, which is neither persecuted nor reviled, but simply regarded, largely through its own fault, as a bore. Local churches which are respected and even attended by 'the public'—interpreted as people who under different circumstances would not feel obliged to attend church at all —are often found to be those where, on a Christian judgement, the gospel seems to be most faithfully preached. Such churches may invite and suffer temporary periods of unpopularity—by standing up for West Indian immigrants, say, or refusing indiscriminate baptism. But on the whole, the storms are weathered by churches, and ministers, whose

[1] Albert M. Lyles, *Methodism Mocked* (Epworth Press, 1960).

interest in the community and presentation of the faith is alert and genuine. Even so, the Church has every excuse for getting itself disliked: none at all for escaping notice.

Moreover, those outside Dissent who are interested enough to form an opinion about it (a dwindling company) are very often in a position to know what they are talking about. They, or their parents, are part of the mighty army, running into millions, who have since the turn of the century 'voted with their feet' by leaving the chapels their ancestors attended. Their reasons for going are legion, and mostly private to them: ask them why they went and they might tell you, if they were articulate people, what they honestly believed was the truth, but it would not necessarily be so. Man is a poor examiner of his own motives. But the true reasons, in so far as they can be ascertained or suspected, are important, and some of them are at least respectable enough to occasion a little more self-criticism in the deserted chapels than is commonly heard there.

Of course, it is not suggested that ex-Nonconformists have a monopoly of the 'respectable' reasons for abandoning organized religion altogether, or seeking different forms of it from those in which they were brought up. All the non-Roman denominations have been severely depleted since what are popularly regarded as the religious boom years during the latter half of the last century. We expect too much if we expect ever to know precisely why, but some of the causes are comparatively clear-cut, like the impact of Biblical criticism and the popularization of scientific knowledge—an impact which naturally fell more severely on those to whom religion meant 'Bible' than on those to whom it meant 'sacrament'.

Other causes, no less influential even though much less easily comprehended, are perhaps to be found in what Raymond Williams calls 'the structure of feeling'[1]—the whole

[1] *The Long Revolution* (Chatto, 1961), pp. 48–9.

mélange of moral attitudes, linguistic usages, communal and personal priorities, moods, ideas, pleasures, whose subtle, perpetual changes mark the difference between one generation or decade and the next. Sometimes the changes are minor, holding a country or a civilization steady for a time while behind there pile up tremendous upheavals that anyone can recognize—a Renaissance, a Reformation. Even then, recognition of such an event, or at least of its implications, may come much later—too late for the organism chiefly affected to do much about ensuring its own survival in the new world which has been created. Thus, Rome tagged along with the Renaissance, employing its greatest artists, electing some of its characteristic figures to the Papacy. But she could not recognize in the lines of Michelangelo's Adam, painted on the Sistine Chapel ceiling, the pattern of the new man and the new, unacceptable demands which he would make of her.

The situation of the Free Churches is not of this order of significance, and outside this country it would be of only marginal interest but for the world-wide confessions which have sprung from English soil. But the years 1870-1914, and perhaps the lesser period 1945 to the present day, may have been requiring changes in Dissenting thought, practice and organization at least as great as those which would have been needed in the Church of England for that body to anticipate the Methodist revival, and make John Wesley's ordinations unnecessary.

Clearly, no less radical changes have been required of the Church of England too in the present century, and only a few of them have been forthcoming. But not the same changes. Of late, the cold winds of secularism which have been blowing round the Church, and the warm breath of ecumenicity inside it, have encouraged commentators to lump 'the Churches' together and write as though all their problems were the same. For a very long time—say, from Shakespeare's 'I had as lief be a Brownist as a politician' to Wilde's 'There is nothing in the whole world so unbecoming to a woman as a Nonconformist conscience'—it was indeed Dissent which occupied in the English religious scene the place reserved for things 'not done'. Now, though churchgoing has again become modish in certain sections of society, generally speaking it is Christianity itself which is 'not done', and the ecclesiastical ranks have been closing. It is a good thing, because the Churches cannot solve their problems apart. But they cannot start solving them until each denomination has separately understood and accepted the predicament it is in, and prepared itself at every level for radical change.

I have already summed up the Free Churches' predicament as lack of freedom. This paradoxical-sounding position must now be expanded. It may fairly be set against the judgement of Dr Ernest Payne, written nearly twenty years ago :

> 'It is difficult to see how a church which is State-established, and regards episcopal government and liturgical services as essential to its life, can give sufficient freedom to comprehend within itself the spontaneous, vigorous and varied expressions of the gospel which have been created by the Free Church tradition.'[1]

Dr Payne, a Baptist scholar and a leader of the World Council of Churches, is a sterner critic of his own tradition than this somewhat idealized passage suggests. The Free Churches, as they stand at the Ejectment tercentenary, are in no position to claim against the Church of England that *their* tradition is spontaneous, vigorous and varied : 'mechanical, limp, and monotonous' are adjectives which would represent the truth almost as nearly. After all, in what is the freedom of the Free Churches usually held to consist? Is it not, first, the freedom to construct for each occasion of worship a flexible and spontaneous (though not anarchic) liturgical offering; second, the freedom to make organization follow life, to discover in each generation an

[1] *The Free Church Tradition*, p. 184.

ecclesiastical structure conformable to the Word of God and the needs of the time; third, the freedom to range through English society, asserting the gospel's judgement on the established order without being inhibited by State patronage or protection? And what has happened to these freedoms in practice?

Free in Worship?

Of all these freedoms, the freedom of worship probably looms largest in the mind of the average chapelgoer (if he exists). Yet one of the principal features of our worship as it actually is in the vast majority of churches is its bondage to a stereotype, its conspicuous lack of variety, between different denominations, between different churches of the same denomination, and between the different services of any given church. The shibboleth 'Unity not uniformity', still on the lips of some Free Church orators when they are invited to contemplate Reunion, has become farcical in a liturgical con- text, for uniformity is what we already have. This lack of variety—the slavish adherence to leaden hymn-sandwiches on all possible occasions—is in itself enough to discourage any healthy-minded person from going to church twice in one day, or even twice in one week. But more important is the spiritual deadness to which it calls attention. The Free Churches came into being, one remembers wrily, in part be- cause they wanted to be able to order their worship as they saw fit. Today, the freedom they won is extensively enjoyed by others. When Anglicans or even Roman Catholics tire of the great riches available to them in their own set liturgies, they are still able to write their own prayers, at least for informal occasions, or sing hymns written by Dissenters. The Dissenters themselves have long been too hot against Popery to explore what was good in pre-Reformation practice, and have lacked the wit to devise or adopt anything new. How often does one meet in a chapel a service constructed round one of the simpler Bach cantatas, or a celebration of the

Eucharist according to the rite of the Church of South India? They are only just beginning to recover for general use the tradition of order and dignity, derived from Geneva, which they were happy to use in the seventeenth century; and at the same time they are rapidly losing the freedom of expression in worship, freedom to 'follow the Spirit where it listeth', which was enjoyed by the Puritans and the Primitive Methodists, and before them by the New Testament Church.

Yet it is widely and rather curiously believed, both within and without Dissenting congregations, that the tradition of 'free prayer', as offered in their midst, is by itself enough to preserve this Puritan freedom of expression. Free prayer, nowadays most carefully and conscientiously prepared rather than extempore, is still the general custom in the Free Churches. But it is doubtful whether it any longer conveys an impression of freedom to those who are invited to worship through it. In any church it is easy to see that the younger members of the congregation find the rotund phrases and loose sentence structure of the old style difficult to make their own, and for many of them free prayer is not what it is for some of their elders—a defensive mark of distinction from the supposed formality of other traditions. Many of them have been introduced at school and elsewhere to the wide variety of modern as well as ancient written prayers. Even those who have not been are far more accustomed, in secular society, to variants on ritual forms than to the slow accumulations of consecutive speech and argument. (The form—as opposed to the style and content—of certain pop songs and advertisements might repay study in this connection.) Free Church ministers have been slow to introduce to their congregations the merits of responsive and bidding prayers, and their only concession in worship to the habits of the world they live in has been their intense dislike of silence.

Silence, indeed, is the one form of worship which is almost universally thought intolerable by Dissenting clergy. Despite their not-too-distant affinity to the Quakers, they think they will be heard for their much speaking. And since their organists too are equally reluctant to let any liturgical action pass without a ruminative obbligato on the Swell manual, congregations are subjected to unrelieved noise during a service which may well have begun with the reading of the sentence, 'Be still, and know that I am God.'

There are other difficulties which beset prayer in public worship, as it is attempted in the Free Churches. Speaking in public, or rather the old formal style in which this used to be done, has gone out of fashion. Between Gladstone or Lloyd George addressing a public meeting, and a Nonconformist minister addressing the Almighty, there used to be a perceptible link of style, and the Puritans themselves skipped quite naturally from public oratory to public prayer. But there is now no accepted oratorical style which can readily be adapted for public prayer, with its thee's and thou's, and God forbid that any minister should solve the problem by imitating Mr Macmillan's approach to a television talk (though a conversational style, preferably copied from different sources, is obviously quite appropriate for sermons). In fact, almost all the prayer actually offered from Free Church pulpits is in one sense only reverent and entirely sincere pastiche, and to this extent not 'free'. Its virtue to the modern ear—and it is a very real virtue—is its topicality rather than its spontaneity.

Even so, the tragedy of contemporary Dissenting worship lies elsewhere. The great strength of the 'free' tradition did not lie in its public manifestations at all—hence the ignorance of it almost always displayed by otherwise enlightened Anglicans—but in its private and semi-public occasions: family prayers, church or class meetings, the gatherings of a few believers for collective intercession. The development of this domestic piety was encouraged in the early days by official prohibition of public meetings for worship, and it survived without too many damaging changes into the twentieth century, though by 1900 parts of the tradition had coarsened or worn thin. But now, family prayers have gone almost beyond recall. Congregational and Baptist church meetings, though nearly every informed member of these denominations insists that there must be a renewal here and that he personally can see one, have nevertheless in general been corrupted into mere business meetings, attended by about a fifth of the membership and no longer devoted to worship on an intimate scale, shading naturally into conversation in the presence of God about the faith and its implications for the particular company of believers present. House groups for worship and Bible study, though they have the official blessing of the World Council of Churches, are still the exception rather than the rule in chapel fellowships.

In short, it is no longer normal for a Free Church layman to express himself aloud to God, or even about God, in the hearing of his fellows, and the 'freedom' of Dissenting worship has not succeeded in overcoming the sense of reserve imposed by sociological and cultural factors. In so far as successful attempts are being made to reverse this degenerative process, the attempts are not peculiar to the Free Churches. Thus, the Orthodox Dissenting denominations have of late been compelled by shortage of ministers and reluctance to close or group redundant or weak churches to take more seriously than ever before the training of lay preachers. (The Methodists have from their earliest times relied heavily on this form of service.) But at the same time Anglicans too have been greatly expanding their lay readership. That there is still some gap between the powers of self-expression possessed by lay Anglicans and lay Dissenters I do not deny, but the gap is narrowing.

It would be quite unfair to imply that nothing has been done to raise the Free Churches from a liturgical and theological nadir which was in fact reached many years ago. In a good many Dissenting chapels and colleges there has been since the forties or thereabouts what amounts to a revolution in the conduct and content of public worship—more properly a counter-revolution, restoring what had once been possessed, and later lost. There are now even a few churches where it is permissible for the congregation to say amen to the prayers ! Writers of books and articles on the Free Churches now almost invariably refer to this recovery of the Reformed liturgy, and the recovery is part of a liturgical and theological renewal which has invaded most of Christendom in recent years, Rome included.

Less often, however, do such writers make it clear just how seldom this or indeed any other self-consistent and Biblical form of worship is to be found in its full purity and glory in a Free church. No Anglican, at least in an urban area, has to drive more than a few miles to find a church where his services are decently and imaginatively conducted (his conscience may direct his feet towards his own parish church, which may or may not be satisfactory, but that is another matter). A Free Churchman seeking a service at which he can be sure of finding no sentimental trimmings patched on to the original simplicities, even at which he can know that the existence of the Old Testament will be acknowledged, is in very much worse case. A man who spends a Sunday or two touring chapels in Bradford, or Wiltshire, or Stoke-on-Trent, will swiftly come to the conclusion that a liturgical tradition which was born free has yet to lose the chains loaded on it by the irresponsible private judgement of past, and in some cases present, generations.

Free in Church Order?

The second freedom of the Free Churches I described (here following H. W. Clark and Ernest Payne) as the freedom 'to make organization follow life, to discover in each generation ecclesiastical structures conformable to the Word of God and the needs of the time.'

In theory this freedom exists, in the sense that the Free Churches are not at the mercy of Parliament when they want to reform themselves (though it took an Act of Parliament to dispose of the property trusts when the splintered pieces of Methodism were stuck together thirty years ago, and further radical change in the constitution of Methodism would be a complex and intimidating job). But by itself, this freedom means little. It is only meaningful if in practice the Free Churches are better at making organization follow life than the 'control group'—the Church of England, which lacks the theoretical freedom. Certainly, there has in recent years been a great spring-cleaning within individual Dissenting denominations. Creaky though their machinery still is, and exceedingly vulnerable to anyone with a mind to obstruct it, its deficiencies may be seen in perspective by those who are able to recall the picture presented by Methodism before Union, by Congregationalism before the establishment of the Home Churches Fund (1947), or by the Baptist communion before the appointment of its first superintendent. Nor can the Church of England be accused of a hectic appetite for novelty. But in a century which has seen changes ranging from the establishment of the Church Assembly and parochial church councils to the extra-parochial pioneering of the Sheffield Industrial Mission, there is no case for saying that the Free Churches have the secret of self-reformation while the Church of England does not.

We are perhaps better able than our Victorian predecessors to see why this is so, for in sociology we have acquired a new lens through which to examine ourselves. Theologically, we know now that all the different types of church government which we affect—congregational, presbyterian, episcopal— were present in some form or other in the Early Church. To this knowledge we are able to add that all these forms of government, however seemingly free to the break-out of the Holy Spirit, are equally exposed to the stranglehold of institutionalism. By this I do not mean merely conservatism, though this is a very powerful associated force, but the pressure generated by the institution as such in a society so complex and centralized that effectiveness belongs to institutions, and—as the Congregationalists have been discovering—no local church is an island, entire of itself. (Not that a local church, however isolated from its neighbours, is in any way free from institutional pressures in its own life.)

The major Free Church denominations are not particularly good sources for the study of institutionalism in its pure forms. One needs to go, as Mr Bryan Wilson has recently done, to a comparatively new, 'spirit-led' Pentecostal sect like the Elim Four Square Gospel to realize how quickly religion is infiltrated by bureaucracy.[1] (It appears, for instance, that there is a regulation forbidding Elim ministers to court their future wives in the town where they are working—a prohibition, desirable or not, which has not yet been laid on the ministries of older denominations.) In the Free Churches the processes are more complex, because the dimension of history is much more significant. Nothing could be less 'conformable to the needs of the time' than the present organizational pattern of the Methodist ministry, but it is historical sentiment, rather than institutional inertia, which keeps it in being.

The use of the ministry is clearly very much in point for a discussion of the relation between organization and life, but I return to it in another chapter. For a sphere in which the ecclesiastical institution, allied to historical, social and theological forces, constricts the gospel and prevents it from meeting the needs of the time, one has only to go to the Free Church use of Sunday. The English—and even more the Scottish or the Welsh—Sunday is popularly regarded as the one institution in this island which has never been captured back from the Puritans. The Lord's Day Observance Society, which despite its large contingent of Anglican Evangelicals quaintly supposes itself to stand in the Puritan tradition, naturally encourages this misconception. But I am speaking here of the use to which Dissenters themselves put Sunday, rather than of their attitude to the unbelieving public's use of it for re-

[1] *Sects and Society* (Heinemann, 1961).

creation. This we can indeed trace back to the Puritans, whose celebration of Sunday was a counterblast to the hagiological excesses of Rome and the unreformed sections of the English Church. A calendar of days sacred to improbable saints, and marked as much by guzzling as by genuflection, had become in Puritan practice a weekly summons to hear the gospel proclaimed on the day of the Lord's Resurrection. All other festivals—even Christmas—were secondary, and after 1662 Sunday observance became and remained one of the chief symbols of Dissenting solidarity. Dissenters' attendance at field meeting or chapel, not once but twice a Sunday, was what marked them off as a community, oppressed but visibly a force to be reckoned with. Their sober behaviour for the rest of the day merely reinforced this impression.[1]

This pattern of worship, and the Dissenting social cohesion which went with it, has long since been broken. Comparatively few contemporary Free Churchmen go to church more than once a Sunday, and while some ministers still speak as though two attendances were, or should be, the norm, others are heard complaining that their morning and evening congregations never meet each other. The carriage-and-pair or the bridled farm-horse at the chapel door has become the family saloon parked on the beach 'away from it all', and who is to say that in the hurly-burly of modern urban life both forms of refreshment are not equally necessary, especially if a family is together at no other time?

Bishop Leslie Hunter, himself the son of a Free Church minister, has blamed 'the passing of the Puritan Sabbath' for 'the sad decline in the vigour of Free Church worship', on the grounds that the change left Free Churchmen with no alternative discipline of worship. For the insight that freedom and vigour in worship are in some sense dependent on disci-

---

[1] After all, this aspect of sabbath observance was not confined to Dissenters. 'Sunday travelling had not been uncommon' wrote Jane Austen in *Persuasion* of a character whom she wished to exhibit as a sad rake.

pline we may be grateful. But cause and effect are hard to distinguish here. A community whose worship was vigorous might have seen the re-creation rather than the passing of the Puritan Sabbath, at least in the lives of its own members. But, unhappily, the present typical pattern of Dissenting Sunday worship—services at 11 a.m. and 6.30 p.m., afternoon Sunday School (now, it is true, gradually being exchanged for morning 'family church'), and monthly communion service—seems to have become fixed at a time when Sabbath observance was already beginning to be eroded, and this has probably helped to make any proposed break in the routine extremely distasteful.

People who have guiltily let slip—rather than consciously forsaken—the practice of their fathers do not like to be reminded of the fact by settling down to appraise the changes which time and social revolution have made necessary. How many chapels in Britain are prepared, like some of their livelier American counterparts, to hold a single Sunday service at 9 a.m. during the summer months and recognize their people's desire to go out for the rest of the day? (The change in many Anglican parishes from Matins to Parish Communion, though undertaken for liturgical rather than pragmatic reasons, has in fact brought them closer into line with social realities.) Are the Free Churches, let alone the professional sabbatarians in their midst, really *free* to think through the change in the use of Sunday which is imposed by British industry's need to work its automatic machines round the clock?[1] It is our history, and our social status, not our theology, which makes us feel we are surrendering to secularism if we change anything. But who knows what we might gain if the worship of God were brought into our

---

[1] One recalls the Methodist chapel in one of the Welsh steel mill towns, which steadfastly refused to alter its time of evening worship, although the time in question straddled a shift changeover; and specifically excluded from attendance some two-thirds of the town's working population.

weekday lives, where it belongs, and if downtown chapels were no longer bolted and barred between weekly attempts to lure a totally alienated society inside?

Free in Witness to Society?

The third freedom to which the Free Churches make explicit or implicit claim I described as 'the freedom to range through English society, asserting the gospel's judgement on the established order, without being inhibited by State patronage or protection'.

I have deliberately phrased this loosely, because the freedom it describes is loosely understood by most Free Churchmen. After all, no Christian, Anglican or Roman or Dissenter, is prevented from saying what he likes about any aspect of this country's established order, whether it is Prince Philip's polo-playing, television violence or the Suez war, and an Anglican vicar, especially, is politically accountable to no one except his Maker. But viewed collectively, Dissent and the Church of England do have very different places in society, and Dissent has historically tended to see itself as Micaiah, while casting the Church of England for the multiple role of the five hundred false prophets, who told King Ahab only what he wanted to hear.

If this sketch of how Dissent feels about itself is justified, three questions arise. The first is whether the Free Churches have ever enjoyed this aspect of their freedom as fully as they think they have. The second is whether they possess it now, and if not, whether they can recover it. I think the answers to these questions are—in order—'No', 'No', 'Possibly'. In this chapter, I only attempt to comment on the first two.

We may admit straight away that in ordering their church government, in campaigning for their civil liberties, and in their enforced separation from the seats of patronage and ultimate political power, the Dissenters displayed great determination and skill in exploiting and extending those democratic processes to which they had access. But at no time since the Restoration have they constituted a philosophically dangerous critique of English society's basic structure. Once William of Orange was on the throne, the Puritans could set about demonstrating their loyalty—suspect as far back as the 1560s—to the monarchy. It took them a little time to become what they are now, one of that institution's most reliable props, but once the Hanoverians were in, loyal duty and self-interest marched together.

The point may be briefly illustrated from several different periods in the history of the Free Churches. First, it is important to remember that the 2,000-odd clergy whose expulsion from the Established Church in 1662 created the Free Churches as institutions were by no means all strikingly different in political and social outlook from their brethren who sat snugly in their vicarages. The revolutionaries who emerged during the Commonwealth and had their memorable say in the Army debates at Putney were treated more tolerantly by Cromwell than they would have been by Archbishop Laud, but this does not mean that their political philosophy commended itself to Cromwell's supporters.

In the next century, it is instructive to note the composition of the committee of Protestant Dissenting Deputies, set up in 1738 to campaign in and out of Parliament for the removal of Dissenters' civil disabilities. It was naturally in the interest of Dissent to elect as weighty a committee as possible; even so, it would be a rare Christian committee these days which could assemble quite so many pillars of the Bank of England. The first chairman, Samuel Holden, was himself Governor of the Bank and of the Russia Company, an MP, and a supporter of Walpole. He died leaving £80,000 —close on a millionaire at today's prices.[1]

But for the clearest and most detailed available picture of

---

[1] N. C. Hunt, *Two Early Political Associations* (Oxford, 1961), p. 202.

the politics and sociology of Free Churchmen in a particular place over a long period, we have to go to E. R. Wickham's *Church and People in an Industrial City* (Sheffield). There we are reminded that it was not the Ejectment, nor the Methodist revival (the work of a High Church Tory), which brought the urban and rural poor into long-standing and intimate connection with the Church, but the later Methodist schisms forced by popular distaste for the snobbish and reactionary Wesleyans. This is how Wickham describes the Old Dissenters (Congregationalists, Baptists, Presbyterians and Unitarians) as they appeared in Sheffield at the time of the French Revolution:

> Their long experience of political disability as well as theological attitude predisposed them to political reform, in an age that was stirred by such possibilities. But also they had prospered in their callings, and particularly in the non-chartered towns like Sheffield where they had taken strongest root, and were among the leading manu- facturers. If on some scores they were drawn to support democratic causes ... on other scores they could have an instinctive and shrewd fear of democracy, not to speak of revolution, that challenged them as a socially privileged group. Both elements and the tensions between them per- sisted, and continued in the heart of the Liberal Party of the nineteenth century, which was so strongly sustained by Radical Nonconformity.[1]

These tensions, it might be added, were well illustrated by the attitude of the Old Dissenters to, respectively, the anti- Corn Law agitation and the Factories Acts. Generally speak- ing, they were aroused to an impressive pitch of humani- tarian indignation about the hungry labourers who could only be fed by the introduction of Free Trade, but as indi- vidualists and Free Traders themselves, they refused to ally themselves with Anglican and Methodist evangelicals like Shaftesbury and Oastler in seeking legislation to protect child

[1] (Lutterworth Press, 1957), p. 68.

workers in factories.[1] But even the Primitive Methodists—
the group which chiefly made it possible for Morgan Phillips
to say that the Labour Party 'owed more to Methodism than
to Marxism', and which reached further down into the social
strata than any other denomination—had a strong strain of
political passivity and commercial respectability. As Bishop
Wickham says,

> The Primitive Methodist picture in Sheffield in the latter
> half of the nineteenth century is of a denomination largely
> made up of the most respectable of the working class, al-
> ways appearing well-dressed, devout, enthusiastic, and
> even in places 'corybantic' in their worship, with an ad-
> mixture of the lower middle group, small tradesmen and
> such people; not without a handful of wealthier families
> in some chapels, who had made money and retained their
> old associations ... it is certain that the great bulk of the
> poorer workmen and their wives were not thronging the
> chapels.[2]

By the end of the nineteenth century, the Unitarian
Charles Booth's famous inquiry into *London Life and Labour*
was revealing what a contemporary reviewer described as
'a decadence in ecclesiastical Christianity'. Booth's biogra-
phers, T. S. and M. B. Simey, here comment:

> This was especially true in so far as the working classes
> hardly came under the direct influence of the churches at
> all, whereas, at the time at least, they were very ready to
> follow the lead of socialist politicians, especially those at
> the head of the trade unions which were then rapidly
> growing in power. Furthermore, Booth was able to demon-
> strate in considerable detail that the decline in religious
> influence was due in some measure at least to social and
> economic factors. Religious institutions had become so dis-
> connected from the wider society in the life of which they

[1] Cf. Raymond Cowherd, *The Politics of English Dissent*
(Epworth Press, 1959), p. 144.
[2] *Op. cit.*, p. 134.

should have participated, that the endeavours of individuals of goodwill, intelligence and even saintliness had ceased to exert anything like the decisive influence which might have stemmed the rising tide of disillusion.[1]

Of course, as the Simeys (themselves Christian sociologists) point out, the position of the churches at that time is now thought of as the most prosperous which organized Christianity in this country has ever enjoyed.

This picture of Dissent's past is unashamedly partial, and there are parts of the country (South Wales is a case in point) where it is untrue to the facts. The picture is presented as a corrective to the view—not uncommon among Dissenters even today—that Liberal Nonconformity had all the virtues of the Labour Party without any of its vices, and that Socialist intellectuals' distrust of Dissent is without foundation. It makes it possible to question the much-quoted judgement of Professor D. W. Brogan in *The English People*: 'Religious dissent, accompanied by hardships that are serious but not demoralizing, is good education in real radicalism' ...[2] The hardships, latterly at any rate, were not serious, and the radicalism did not go to the roots. In the eighteenth and early nineteenth centuries, Dissent was too cohesive and self-sufficient an institution for its members to feel individually ill-treated because they could not get themselves flogged by Keate, skinned at White's, or liquored at the Bullingdon.

Their social discontent was corporate rather than personal. When the Protestant Dissenting Deputies recorded, as they frequently had to, their displeasure at the refusal of an Anglican vicar to bury a Dissenter's child, their indignation was primarily concerned not with the feelings of the parents but with the honour due to their religion; nor did there exist professionally sentimental national newspapers to assert different priorities. It was a great thing for English society

[1] *Charles Booth, Social Scientist* (Oxford, 1960), p. 237.
[2] (*London* 1943), p. 126.

in its period of rapid expansion that the most able Dissenters did not covet inordinately individual promotion and aristocratic flummery, but stayed in the places which had made them prosperous, content with local repute and national anonymity. Had they behaved differently, English local government, which is largely their creation, would not have received its solid nineteenth century grounding, and we would have had to wait a few more decades for our drains. But abstinence from top people's pleasures, though it may build character, does not make a radical. By the end of the last century Dissenters had an enormous stake in social stability, and there is symbolic aptness in the minute recorded in 1908 by the Dissenting Deputies, expressing displeasure because they had not been invited to the Royal garden party.

They were, in fact, already on parole not to disturb the established order, and except here and there, through their ecumenical connections or through individuals, they have not broken parole yet. One has only to contemplate the present state of the alliance between Nonconformity and the Liberal Party. As everyone knows who has met the Liberals recently, they are now not one party but two; a party of old people and young people, conservatives and radicals, people from dying rural communities and people from brisk modern suburbs. With distinguished exceptions, the remaining Nonconformists in the party belong to the first of all these pairs.[1]

It is much the same with Methodism and the Labour Party. In a sense, indeed, Methodism is now a positive handicap to Labour, for the people in the party who are closest both in

[1] It is only fair to add that the survival of the Liberal Party at all must in part be ascribed to the intense loyalty of its Non-Conformist members – loyalty only comparable, in its docile acceptance of setbacks, with the loyalty which they lavish on their chapels. And perhaps nowadays there is a budding correlation between the growth of Liberalism in the Home Counties and the strength of chapels in similar localities.

background and outlook to the chapels tend to be the rows of extinct trade unionists who sit in Parliament for the safest Labour seats in the country, and saddle their colleagues with the image of cosy antediluvianism.

Does Dissent then have, socially speaking, a hopeless task? That remains to be seen. What is certain is that it is sheer romanticism to think it possible for Dissent ever again to exert the kind of collective impact on society which it did up to 1914. That depended on a depth of cultural roots, and an intimacy of contact nationally and locally between leaders and led, which does not now exist. Now, any Nonconformist denomination can and sometimes does produce a significant report, or sound a call to action, in the certain knowledge that 99 out of 100 church members will never heed it; and the established order is not disturbed by an attacking force which consists largely of generals. The freedom to initiate and supervise social change, which has been at least latent and from time to time patent in the Free Church tradition, is not now vested in the Free Churches as such.

However, it may still belong locally to that minority of chapels whose material and spiritual strength is adequate to this further task. (It naturally belongs also to individual Dissenters who are prepared to transmit what they know and are through the existing institutions of secular society and the developing institutions of the ecumenical movement.) Obviously the role of new churches in private and municipal housing estates is vital here, and it is a pity that it is these churches, short as they so often are of money or leadership or both, that are most handicapped by the deep weaknesses and timidities of the denominations which support them.

Nevertheless, the churches are there, in areas of (for England) rapid social change. They will succeed if their members are granted what has always been a Dissenting rather than an Anglican virtue: a quick and instinctive perception of people's half-realized needs, and of the direction in which a new social group is moving. From this could emerge a style of Dissenting life—and worship—which was both distinctive and relevant. Even if this happens—and it is hard to be sanguine about it—society might recognize only slowly, if ever, the contribution which chapels as such were making to its well-being. But we must accustom ourselves to that. We have long enough made the mistake of expecting other people to accept us at our own valuation.

II

THE IMAGE OF PURITANISM

Here is an abridged list in alphabetical order of epithets which have been hurled at the Society's secretary:

Bigot	Fanatic	Prude
Blue Nose	Grundy	Puritan
Busybody	Judas	Sabbatarian
Chadband	Kill Joy	Snooper
Crank	Miser	Stiggins
Crazy	Meddlesome	Twerp
Dictator	Mugwump	Tyrant
Dismal Jimmy	Nosey Parker	Wowser

The Lord's Day Magazine, No 197 (Oct.-Dec. 1950), p. 46.

Most of us think that we do know all about Puritanism. But too often we are thinking—whether with conscious hostility or unconscious sympathy—not of Puritanism at all but of later nonconformity. They differ as much as vinegar does from wine.—
Christopher Hill, preface to *Puritanism and Revolution* (Secker & Warburg, 1958).

In the previous chapter, I made use from time to time of the word 'Puritan'. It is a hard word to avoid in discussing what has gone towards the making of the Free Churches, but it is an equally hard one to use in the neutral, unselfconscious tone of voice suitable for descriptive historical terms. The reasons for this are obvious enough. As the Oxford Dictionary indicates, ever since the 1560s 'Puritan' and its derivatives have been used in a highly-coloured, almost universally pejorative sense to denote any person or attitude by which the speaker feels himself to be rebuked. Originally, the rebuke intended and felt was theological. The first English Puritans were Elizabethan Anabaptists and Independents, 'pure unspottyd Lambes of the Lord', who wanted the reform of the Church to go much further than it had done. Now, as the Lord's Day Observance Society's list of synonyms shows, the rebuke felt is moral and cultural.

But because the Puritans abused were a significant group in their own right—like Whigs and Tories—the word has another role in the English vocabulary. It is used by educated people simply to describe this group: a political, ecclesiastical, social and economic 'interest', which coagulated during the reign of Elizabeth I and came to power in the seventeenth century. This use of the word has been extended to cover the kind of qualities and culture which can be regarded as characteristic of the Puritan section of English society, and this is the use with which I am chiefly concerned here. It took on a new lease of life at the Old Bailey in 1961, when Mr Richard Hoggart told a sadly puzzled prosecuting counsel that *Lady Chatterley's Lover* was 'highly virtuous if not puritanical', and went on to say:

Many people live their lives under a misapprehension of the word 'puritanical'. This is the way in which language decays. In England today and for a long time, the word 'puritanical' has been extended to mean somebody who is against anything which is pleasurable, particularly sex. The proper meaning of it, to a literary man or to a linguist, is somebody who belongs to the tradition of British puritanism generally, and the distinguishing feature of that is an intense sense of responsibility for one's conscience. In this sense this book is puritanical.[1]

What Was Puritanism?

Some of us were surprised to read such a careful definition of Puritanism which nevertheless skated round its Christian

[1] *The Trial of Lady Chatterley*, ed. Rolph (Penguin, 1961), p. 99.

point of departure. Others, of course, were much more surprised to see their image of Mrs Grundy so suddenly meta-
morphosed into open-hearted Connie Chatterley. All of us,
Mr Hoggart included, are to some extent victims of this un-
shakable tenet of English pseudo-history: that the typical
Puritan worshipped a small-minded, teetotal, colourless God
who hated nothing more than seeing his children enjoying
themselves. Yet it is not merely school history books and their
more ignorant expositors which have kept this lie alive, but
the endurance right up to the present day in our society of
sharp differences over the role which conscience ought to play
in the entire spectrum of human behaviour, in worship,
politics, art, morals. During the seventeenth century these
differences hardened into rigid social, political and ecclesiastical structures, and because some of the structures are now
crumbled or defaced out of all recognition, people find it
hard to account for the endurance, albeit in new forms, of the
old disputes.

This, I think, is why Christians should not be too irritated
by the developing use of 'Puritan' as an intellectual vogue-
word, not only in the Cambridge English school where it has
long been familiar, but in the weightier Sunday newspapers
as well. For in Puritanism we have a priceless symbol through
which to comprehend the process of change, decay and division in English religion and English culture. Moreover, the
future of the Free Churches, and of the way of life which
in their better moments they seek to reproduce, is deeply
involved in this exercise in semantic archaeology. For in dig-
ging for the truth about Puritanism there are several layers
of unlovely Victorian potsherds to be penetrated first, and
it is in some sense due to the presence of these layers that
Puritanism, in so far as it is a living force in contemporary
Britain, is bypassing the religious institutions which were in
at its birth.

This is why a discussion of Puritanism must take account
of 'the Nonconformist conscience', a phrase which came into

common usage towards the end of the last century and which, in most of its remaining overt expressions, can be regarded as Puritanism in decay. Naturally, it is not generally so regarded among Free Churchmen. A few months ago I attended an ecumenical conference where a young, acute and progressive Methodist minister said in the course of a paper on interchurch relations that the Methodists, by virtue of their 'witness' on drink and gambling, were to be thought of as 'the residuary legatees of Puritan morality'. It is not only Methodists among Dissenters who make this kind of assumption. Of course, if this is really all that there is left of the legacy, it is hardly worth turning up at the solicitor's to hear the will read. But it is not quite as bad as that.

However, before proceeding further, it is necessary to obtain a clearer picture of the sort of people the Puritans themselves were, and of the beliefs which informed their behaviour.[1] The religious mainspring of the Puritan character was its sense, derived from John Calvin, of God's immeasurable majesty and righteousness. This led instantly to a strong sense of sin, of man's shame and littleness before God, and of personal responsibility for what was done in God's sight. Many Christians and almost all secular commentators are unaware that there was anything more to the religion of the Puritans than this highly-developed consciousness of sin. But the enormous creativity—social, intellectual, and aesthetic—which characterized Puritans from Baxter to Locke, Milton to Gainsborough, Bunyan to Elizabeth Fry, sprang ultimately from the realization that this hyper-awareness was meant as a tool to salvation rather than as a crushing burden of guilt, that in Christ God had redeemed the sinner and set him free to work and worship joyfully in the here and now. Hence the note of victory and thanksgiving sounded by the great Puritans. But they were dependent on God's grace for their continued share in his victory, and they

[1] The following paragraph leans heavily on an unpublished address by the Rev. Daniel Jenkins.

were sure that sin was constantly making efforts to reclaim its hold upon them.

Here lay the seeds of the corrupted thing which Puritanism latterly became, and which remains its popular image. Conviction of sin led to the habit of self-examination, good in itself, which however was easily transmuted into self-justification and censoriousness. This in turn became overlaid with the individualist pietism which was the least happy aspect of the Methodist and subsequent revivals. Eventually, children—as we may learn from such nineteenth century documents as Samuel Butler's *The Way of All Flesh* and Sir Edmund Gosse's *Father and Son*—were brought up to believe that their only hope of pleasing God was through correctness of belief, or evangelistic fervour, or abstinence from worldly pleasures. Not surprisingly, the children commonly rebelled against the unreality of their upbringing, and its denial of legitimate human experience. They found, and find still, that the world of artistic and scientific achievement is distorted by this attitude, and their essentially Puritan consciences, unless atrophied by total escape into thoughtless hedonism, disown their immediate ancestry in unconscious loyalty to their ultimate origins.

Puritanism, in fact, strode a knife-edge of Christian maturity from which it was easy to fall. What this maturity meant at its best can be discovered from Lucy Hutchinson's *Memoir* of her husband, Colonel Hutchinson, who was the Puritan governor of Nottingham during the Civil War. He died in 1663, and the memoir, discovered and published in 1806, is a work of great charm and tenderness. The tone in which Mrs Hutchinson describes her husband is panegyrical, but it is the qualities approved, and her reasons for approving them, which are significant:

> ... he could dance admirably well, but neither in youth nor riper years made any practice of it; he had skill in fencing, such as becomes a gentleman; he had a great love of music, and often diverted himself with a viol, on which

he played masterly, and he had an exact ear and judgement in other music . . . he had great judgement in paintings, gravings, sculpture and all liberal arts, and had many curiosities of value in all kinds. . . .

His whole life was the rule of temperance in meat, drink, apparel, pleasure, and all those things that may be lawfully enjoyed; and herein his temperance was more excellent than in others, in whom it is not so much a virtue, but proceeds from want of appetite or gust of pleasure; in him it was a true, wise and religious government of the desire and delight he took in the things he enjoyed.[1]

All those things that may be lawfully enjoyed. . . . No wonder Mrs Hutchinson resented the 'court-caterpillars', as she calls them, who branded her husband and his like as 'illiterate, morose, melancholy, discontented, crazed sort of men, not fit for human conversation'. On this latter passage her 1806 editor comments:

Such is the idea entertained of them (the Puritans) in general even at this day; whoever shall read these memoirs will be well convinced that not one of these qualities needs or does by any natural consequence accompany the character.

But of course, most people have not read the memoirs and are not convinced. Besides, it is to the behaviour of institutional Nonconformity over the last two hundred years or so that we must look for the source of the myth which could make a great historian, Halévy, write in 1913: 'If a Puritan merchant deigned to accord any attention to the fine arts, he was actuated not by any aesthetic ideals, but by the hope that the improvement of artistic technique might indirectly improve the processes of industry'.[2] The Free Churches will not make any progress at all with their mission in contemporary society until they make a conscious effort to erase the

[1] *Memoirs of Colonel Hutchinson* (1908 ed.), pp. 22, 34, 81.
[2] *England in 1815* (Benn, paperback ed.), p. 486.

false image of Puritanism which was originally invented by their bitterest enemies, but which they have gradually come to accept as the true one, to be defended at whatever cost in historical truth, sound doctrine or public respect.

As I hope to show, the arts are not the only sphere in which this needs to be done. Nevertheless, we might remind ourselves rather more often than we do that Spenser and Marvell, as well as Milton, were Puritans; that Robert Browne, the founding father of Independency, was also a 'singular good lutenist' and taught his children to play; and that when one of Cromwell's daughters was married they had (according to a contemporary newsletter) 'forty-eight violins and much mirth with frolics, besides mixt dancing'.[1] Anyone who thinks that they had no wine on that occasion forgets that Cromwell, like most Puritans, was no teetotaller. The development of total abstinence as Nonconformity's counterpart to the Jewish circumcision arose out of a particular social situation at a much later date.

However, we should not delude ourselves that our efforts to erase the old image of Puritanism will be much noticed or applauded unless we are prepared to delineate a new one; and although this can only be done through an understanding of what the Puritans were, it depends on a willingness to see them in contemporary dress. Here I select a statement by Daniel Jenkins which I shall set, on the one hand against the qualities admired and the behaviour stressed in the Free Churches today, and on the other against the secular understanding of Puritanism which has recently come into the open. For the Puritan tradition, far more than we are willing to recognize, is a split one, and cannot be comprehended without reference to both its halves. The Free Churches, it

[1] Cf. Percy Scholes, *The Puritans and Music* (Oxford, 1936), and the article of that title in the same author's *Oxford Companion to Music*; also Hugh Martin, *Puritanism and Richard Baxter* (SCM Press, 1954).

could be said, are sub-Puritan in a Christian way, while many of the most admirable people outside them are Puritan in a sub-Christian way.

Mr Jenkins asks:

What, after all, are the qualities which people of radical temper and so-called advanced tastes admire in modern society? They are a zeal for social righteousness; an impatience with distinctions of rank and class; a desire for beauty, not as meaningless adornment but as expressed in the honest use of materials for their true function; sincerity and sensitivity in personal relations; scepticism about traditional myths and symbols, and a sober concern for the evidence; agnosticism about matters where no finality of judgement is possible, and readiness to adjust oneself to a changing world.

But these I would claim are the Puritan virtues.

It is of great interest to compare this with the more loosely phrased manifesto of a 'secular Puritan', Dr Martin Green, who defines in *A Mirror for Anglo-Saxons*[1] the new British type, 'the decent man', which he sees as the replacement for the 'Establishment type, the gentleman ideal' in our society:

What is always essential is its puritanism, taking that to mean a concern with right and wrong so keen as to set the tone of the whole personality, an eagerness to draw sharp, exclusive lines, mapping out as much as possible of the world, a distrust of all connoisseurship in experience, all aestheticism. There is also something lower middle class about this type; it never aims at elegance or magnificence of the aristocratic kind, or bohemian irresponsibility or indecent exposure, or ruthless theorizing; always at decency, marriage, domesticity, filial and parental duties. It is middle-brow, concerned with every subtlety and profundity of truth, but rendering them plainly, relating them always to the great moral imperatives, hostile to all priesthoods and parties and technocracies and esoteric sys-

[1] (*London* 1961), p. 99.

tems. It is all-round responsible, to class, country, civilization; the four-square citizen and human being, self-
exempted from nothing, even by genius. The typical movement of its mind is scrupulous, in bad ways as well as good,
and therefore irritable as well as honourable.

It is not possible in the course of a single chapter to discuss
all the issues raised by these statements. What follows is
based on a few points drawn from both: 'Zeal for social
righteousness ... sincerity and sensitivity in personal relations ... domesticity (as opposed to elegance) ... all-round
responsibility ... sober concern for the evidence ... a concern with right and wrong so keen as to set the tone of the
whole personality.'

Social Conscience

As I hinted in the last chapter, social righteousness as most
British radicals now understand it was not in all ways a cause
beloved of all Puritans in the seventeenth century. It was
the rule of law without aristocratic favour, rather than uni-
versal suffrage, social welfare and economic egalitarianism
to which they aspired. But these are matters of detail:
it would be surprising if radicals wanted the same things
at periods three centuries apart. The Puritans were men of
their time, though on their left wing there were many men
who were far in advance of their time. We have Colonel
Rainborough at Putney:

> For really I think that the poorest he that is in England
> hath a life to live as the greatest he; and therefore truly,
> sir, I think it's clear, that every man that is to live under
> a government ought first to put himself under that govern-
> ment; and ... I should doubt whether he was an English-
> man or no, that should doubt of these things.

But of much greater significance, especially to the Free
Churches in their present condition, was the philosophical
basis of Puritan social morality, and its instinct to claim new

areas of human conduct for the overlordship of God's righteousness. It is a Marxist historian, Mr Christopher Hill, who has most clearly seen the connection here:

> A conspicuous feature of Puritan Calvinism was its cultivation of the sense of sin. Our consciousness of sin must be aggravated before we can hope for divine mercy. We come to faith in Christ through our sense of sin. In modern pulpit usage this desire to convict of sin is aimed at the individual conscience, to urge the individual to change his life. The Puritan preachers attacked the individual conscience too. But they thought, far more than their twentieth century successors, in terms of the *Church*: a Church that was the nation, society. Sins were not merely individual, but national. This called for a change of heart in a number of individuals: but it might also demand a change of institutions, of personnel, of policy, in government. The Puritan denunciation of sin slipped easily into something that was very close to being a demand for a change of government.[1]

So much for what an Anglican writer, Mr Nicolas Mosley, has called 'the Puritan distinction between religious profession and social custom', a distinction which he seemed to blame for the heartlessness of some British colonial policy in the past.[2] One would think that Milton had never written for Cromwell's Government the Manifesto justifying the war against Spain on grounds of Spanish cruelty to the Indians:

> God has made of one blood all nations of men for to dwell on the face of the earth. . . . All great and extraordinary wrongs done to particular persons ought to be considered as in a manner done to all the rest of the human race.[3]

Mr Hill calls this 'the first State paper ever to make a public grievance of the maltreatment of extra-European peoples by a great power', and adds: 'Whatever we may think of the

[1] *Puritanism and Revolution*, p. 257.
[2] *Part-Time Priests?* (Skeffington, 1960), p. 115.
[3] *Prose Works*, vol. ii, pp. 335—6.

motives of the English government, with the blood of count-
less Irishmen still reeking on its hands, there is still great
significance in having the principle of human brotherhood
thus officially proclaimed as one which should guide the
actions of all states.[1]

However, Mr Mosley was right in his way, for the distinction between religious profession and social custom, between
individual and corporate morality, has sunk very deep into
the Free Churches, even though not so deeply as it has sunk
into Evangelicals of all ecclesiastical traditions. The Nonconformist 'social gospellers' of fifty years back, having made
the elementary mistake of forgetting their Calvinism in their
demand for changed institutions, faded away, and it was
a great surprise to many Christians in Britain when the
Baptists—on the whole the most pietistic of the English Free
Churches—raised such a violent and within the limits of the
possible such an effective campaign against Portuguese oppression in Angola.[2] After all, even in the Church of Scotland, the most politically-minded Reformed communion in
Britain, there is a strong section which regards the General
Assembly's fiercely-contested debates on Central Africa as
something of an irrelevance, and is worried by the extent to
which Scottish missions in Central Africa appear to have
become identified with African political aims.[3]

The truth is that there is a considerable difference between
the outlook of the Free Churches as expressed through the
thought and action of their foreign missionaries, and the
attitudes of local chapels at home. This is not a new

[1]*Op. cit.*, p. 149.

[2]The story is told by Len Addicott in *Cry Angola!* (SCM
Press, 1962).

[3]'Many African children', wrote the *Central African Examiner* in 1959, 'undoubtedly receive their first indoctrination of
national sentiment at Church of Scotland schools'. Perhaps the
Examiner would prefer the indoctrination to come from a Com-
munist cell later on?

phenomenon. It was the Free Churches which opened England's eyes to the duty of preaching the gospel overseas, and their most famous missionaries, from the Baptist William Carey to the Congregationalist David Livingstone, were no pietists. To this day, the representatives of Dissent abroad are generally reluctant to keep their religion, their humanity and their political judgement in separate compartments.

No doubt this is partly because the missionary societies have long claimed a high proportion of the most energetic and intelligent Free Churchmen available, as ministers, doctors, and teachers abroad. But perhaps there is another reason. Working among Africans or Indians or Papuans, often in isolated, backward communities, the active Christian, minister or layman, finds himself becoming what Anglican vicars were once able to be—the 'parson' of the community, necessarily involved in what the community thinks and does and feels. Mission field churches may be 'gathered churches' on the traditional Dissenting pattern, in that they consist of Christians gathered out of an alien environment, where the distinction is not between churchman and nominal churchman but between Christian and Hindu or Moslem or pagan. But it is not so fatally easy for them as it is for the 'gathered' churches of England to become self-contained 'interest groups', whose members find it hard to see why their interest in going to church should involve them in affairs which seem remote, large-scale and rather distasteful.

This new, more subtle predisposition to separate religion from life (more subtle, that is, than the frank pietism of the Evangelical ultras) probably helps to account for the *corporate* laggardliness of Dissent in striking to the roots of contemporary social issues in Britain. (To select at random : the treatment of the aged, education at all ages, the management of affluence, commercial influences on culture and communications, the impact on family life of mass re-housing and modern industrial organization.) The Free Churches are compelled, or think they are compelled, to see every problem in terms of individual responsibility. Unlike their Puritan predecessors—and unlike the Church of England—they are afraid of bigness, of the mass society. As a result, they sometimes come perilously close to the MRA bromide 'Change people and you change the world'.

Other influences have also been at work. It is no longer possible to terrify a prospective parliamentary candidate by threatening to withold the Nonconformist vote from him, because the vote is no longer formidable either numerically or organizationally. Congregations have dwindled, and confessional solidarity softened. Besides, there are simply not enough able men and women in the Free Churches today to provide leadership in the ever-expanding fields where leaders are demanded. There are all too few good pastoral ministers, denominational administrators, ecumenical conference-men, and famous apologists; and no single person who is all four simultaneously. Something has to go, and one of the things which tends to go is original thought—as opposed to reflex responses—on social questions. It is wholly to the good that much Dissenting energy in this direction has been channelled into the Social Responsibility department of the British Council of Churches, and into local councils of churches; and in the circumstances it is perhaps surprising that the 'Christian Citizenship' committees of the individual denominations manage to do anything which is not better done elsewhere. They do sometimes so contrive, and the Methodist department is particularly good. But when the ecumenically-minded have been creamed off into less parochial spheres (and this has been happening since COPEC days between the wars), the Free Churches individually are often left in a watery state, stoppered with men whose conception of Christian citizenship begins and ends with the passing of periodic resolutions condemning drink, gambling and *Lady Chatterley*.

If this represented faithfulness to the gospel, the Puritan tradition, or the real needs of Britain today, one would happily overlook the disastrous effect it has on the popular 'image' of Dissent. But it does not—with the result that we are not unpopular, which we probably ought to be in any case, but merely ridiculous. Nor is there much comfort in the fact that whenever this faction has to deliver the goods it is unable to do so. Nothing any Free Churchman can say would now, unassisted, much delay the passage of any Licensing or Gaming Bill the Government cared to bring in.[1] Even in the discussions on the 1959 Education Act, which increased grants to Church schools and provided Dissenters with some sort of a case, the militants were ineffective, because those of their constituents who had not grown totally apathetic to the subject were aware that there were other more urgent and rewarding claims on their energies.

Individually, though, can it be said that a 'zeal for social righteousness' is characteristic of Free Churchmen today? It is hard to be sure, for one has to rely chiefly on impressions. Not everyone who advertises this quality has it, and not everyone who has it advertises it. But there are certain 'outward and visible signs'. Thus, if we take this zeal to include even a wholly a-political bias towards the service of humanity, and survey those who follow what are often (somewhat misleadingly) called vocations, such as teaching, nursing, or social work, we are likely to conclude that the Free Churches do not merely do as well as they did, but better, when account is taken of their dwindling numbers and high average age.

Hospitals still find it pays them to advertise extensively for staff in the columns of Nonconformist weeklies. Besides, the teaching and welfare professions have expanded hugely in this century, drawing their recruits very often from the sons and daughters of chapelgoers whose own limited education had been filled out and made more humane at Sunday school and weeknight meetings. This was all the more possible because the Free Churches did not generally subscribe, as their

[1] Locally, of course, the chapels may still wield power, as the recent Sunday drinking poll in Wales testifies.

social superiors did, to the doctrine that it is a waste of time, or bad form, to educate a woman. Hence those women, of whom Mrs Morel in *Sons and Lovers* is the exemplar, who both owed much and gave much to their chapels, and became the mothers of 'first-generation graduates'; hence, too, the quickness of the Free Churches to take advantage of feminine emancipation (a cause in which they have lately seemed to lose interest). When people complain, as they are fully entitled to do, of the narrow horizons and incurious stolidity which characterize so many Free Church women, not least those from 'respectable' and tolerably-schooled backgrounds, these other side-effects of chapelgoing, traceable in the most unlikely places, must needs be remembered.[1]

However, even when this is said, it is odd that the insights learnt by individual Free Church men and women in the course of their church life and professional work have recently had so little influence either on their own political behaviour, or on the thinking and moods of the Church as a whole. Nonconformists in the last half century or so have seemed almost incapable of generalizing from personal service of their fellow men to public concern with the best interests of the community as a whole, much as the nursing profession—perhaps the resemblance is significant—has since Florence Nightingale's day found it difficult to translate the individual virtues of its members into flexible and compassionate institutional systems. Dissent has become overlaid with an ordinariness, an aggressive privacy, which is almost entirely foreign to the Puritan tradition.

[1] A. Whigham Price in *Congregational Quarterly* (July and October 1956) has deftly cauterized those students of Lawrence, from T. S. Eliot downwards, who have failed to discover easily ascertainable facts about the cultural environment of Eastwood Congregational Chapel and its Literary Society. The primary sources here are Jessie Chambers' memoir D. H. *Lawrence: a Personal Record*; E. T. Lawrence's earliest letters; and the essay 'Hymns in a Man's Life.'

Risking a charge of professional malice, I must insist on the role played, even if only symbolically, by the *Daily Telegraph* in convincing Dissenters that their religion is a private affair of their own, existing independently of their whole way of life, and only publicly exhibited in church. Nowadays, very many Free Churchmen in positions of some responsibility both in their churches and in secular life, read this newspaper which is in its total ambience, social, political and ecclesiastical, profoundly hostile to everything which Dissenters once thought they stood for. And within this symbol there stands another. The *Telegraph*, like various other journals, was the creation of the Berry family, by origin Welsh Congregationalists from Merthyr Tydfil, where the chapel whose organ they paid for may soon be pulled down to make room for a commercial redevelopment of the town centre.

In the circumstances, it is perhaps not really surprising that although at times of stress and clear-cut injustice the old Puritan drives emerge in the Free Churches, the reaction is slow and muddled when the issues are only a little more complex, and patriotic emotions are involved. Suez divided Dissenters almost as evenly as it divided the rest of Britain, and the swiftest, stiffest protest came not from the communions of John Clifford, Silvester Horne and Hugh Price Hughes, but from the establishmentarian portals of the British Council of Churches.

Domesticity

This leads to other qualities which are claimed for Puritanism revived. The key words here are 'domestic' and 'responsible'. The type with which we are concerned, says Mr Green, aims always at 'decency, marriage, domesticity, filial and parental duties'. These aims are shared by a great many people who have little to do with Puritanism in any sense of the word, but there are few English institutions where they are more stressed than in the Free Churches.

Indeed, it is arguable that in the Free Churches, and in the spectrum of society which has felt their influence, these targets are aimed at to the exclusion of other no less desirable objectives, of which social responsibility is one. The intimidating scale of contemporary forces and organisms, besides our consciousness that all we care for is highly vulnerable to a destructive power which we cannot control, encourage us more and more to become private men, seeking our happiness where it may most easily be found, in relationships that are intimate and elemental. The Bible naturally favours this bias towards domestication, but perhaps not as wholeheartedly as is sometimes conveyed by church leaders who write worried and ill-documented letters to *The Times* about the break-up of family life.[1] And in so far as the typical Free Church, or at least the typical flourishing Free Church, is today a suburban institution reflecting at least some of the suburban values, Nonconformity can fairly be said to exalt the practice of domesticity almost to the status of a theological virtue. Certainly the self-insulation of the average churchgoing family within its own four walls (let the Free Church reader ask himself how many of his fellow church-members have ever invited him home) is a noticeable feature of many fellowships. Again, there are undoubtedly many Dissenters among all the young women teachers who marry and retire into private life before they have made even a token attempt to discharge their responsibilities to the society which trained them. Even in the universities, the prevailing atmosphere of Free Church societies is often notably inward-looking. The tone is set by people whose upbringing has made them slow to lay out their own social and professional talents to the best advantage for the benefit of society at large, and quick to capitalize their undoubted talent for family life.

[1] After all: 'If any man come to me, and hate not his father and mother and wife, and children, and brethren, and sisters, yea, and his own life also, he cannot be my disciple' (Luke 14.26).

However, I do not wish to claim that domesticity, particularly Puritan domesticity, is really only a vice after all. Rather, like most Puritan coin, it is a virtue which is easily flipped over on to its vicious obverse; besides, English society these days is not so strong on the domestic virtues that it can afford to bewail too much the failings which may accompany them. Indeed, it is likely to be argued that when 'decency, marriage, domesticity' are under consideration, the division that matters is not between Puritans and others, but between the whole Christian Church and the world, between the ethos of the Mothers' Union and the ethos of William Hickey. But I persist that family life has been, and still is, especially valued by those who stand in the Puritan tradition. Indeed, it would be strange if it were not. The Puritans, with their close attention to the workings of conscience within them, and their constant recourse to Scripture, were bound to set a high value on bringing up children 'in the nurture and admonition of the Lord'. Under oppression, when the family was almost the only unit of congregation legally allowed to Dissenters and the 'house church' (which some Anglicans are now discovering) was the norm of Christian life, the home took on an importance which it rarely had in Royalist circles. In the course of time, it has almost seemed as if family life has taken over the sacramental significance which latter-day sub-Puritans in the Free Churches ceased to look for in the sacraments themselves.

To take one not unimportant example, the typical Dissenter is not a man who sends his children away to boarding school. There are several sociological and historical reasons for this, some creditable and some not, and I only mean to suggest that one reason is (or has been) the general reluctance of chapel-going people to sign away the rights of both home and chapel as the prime formative influence on their children. (As a Dissenter who went to an Anglican public school and liked it, I can perhaps claim to be unbiased in this matter.)

The child of Nonconformist parents today who goes to the

local primary and grammar school may not know the close, religiously impregnated family atmosphere of former years, when Sunday tea was followed not by Huckleberry Hound, but by hymns round the piano.

> In spite of myself, the insidious mastery of song
> Betrays me back, till the heart of me weeps to belong
> To the old Sunday evenings at home with winter outside
> And hymns in the cosy parlour, the tinkling piano our
> guide.[1]

Nor is the same child so likely nowadays to take over more or less entire the tastes and pleasures of his own family circle—indeed, many of today's family tensions are the result of his refusal to do so. Nevertheless, he grows up in the church to which his family belongs, and even if he moves away from it all, socially, geographically and intellectually, this church remains part of what he means by 'home'.

All this has educational implications to which I return in a later chapter. But it is surely possible to see in this close association of child, parents, community, church and school a climate which encourages the growth of that 'all-round responsibility' which Mr Green regards as characteristic of the Puritan temper. Public schools, of course, encourage *esprit de corps*, which is a very different thing. *Esprit de corps* is generated by institutions which have their own momentum, over and above that which the individual imparts to them: this is true of public schools, of regiments, perhaps of parish churches. They encourage the forming of relationships which are easily put down and exchanged for others, or taken up elsewhere.

A chapel depends entirely on the loyalty and responsibility of its members, at the back of whose minds is constantly the knowledge that their minister's salary comes out of their own

---

[1] D. H. Lawrence. Were the poem less well known, how many today would make the correct ascription?

contributions. A formidable quantity of lay service—on however trivial a level—is expected. Promises have to be kept, people's feelings respected. Certainly, no Christian church of any denomination can live for long if all these qualities are totally lacking; and equally, there are plenty of Free Churches whose ministers despair of their members' insensitivity or fecklessness. But the difference exists, and is indeed partly theological, for it is a popular myth, surviving from the corrupt era of the Victorian and Edwardian pulpit barons, that one attends a Free Church as an individual, insulated from one's fellow-worshippers, to 'taste sermons', rather as a Roman Catholic can 'hear Mass' or an Anglican 'make his Communion' without really needing to know that others are doing the same thing in the same place at the same time. On the contrary, it is hard for anyone who has been brought up in the Puritan tradition to attend a particular chapel more than a few times without feeling a sharp interest in its character as a community, together with a curious sense of personal responsibility (even if it is expressed as an intense dislike) for the way the chapel conducts its worship and manages its affairs. It is perhaps inevitable that this collective sense of responsibility should sometimes degenerate into an amalgam of undisciplined and inflexible personal preferences, where people do not so much respect each other's personalities as indulge each other's whims, and the true interests of the chapel are lost in a sentimentalized aversion from 'trouble'.

More Truth Yet

I seem to have been moving towards saying that 'sincerity and sensitivity in personal relations', which in Daniel Jenkins' judgement is a Puritan virtue also admired by modern radicals, is at the same time a virtue which Free Church life encourages even today. I am reluctant to go as far as this. Mr Jenkins himself is surely right about the Puritans: though we may criticize their psychology in many respects, they at least knew better than to treat people as things.[1] Nor need one look further than the plays, books, films and newspaper features written and read today by people of liberal-left inclination to see the same care for human personality. It might be hard to infer this from the casual conversation and social behaviour of an English intellectual—but watch the same intellectual react to, say, an Evelyn Waugh's contemptuous block dismissal of those unfortunates who fall outside the charmed circle of the Catholic gentry.

Granted, too, that the Free Churches are full of nice, decent people. They always have been, and when the novelists' caricatures are cut down to size, one can see that even the maligned Victorian Nonconformists were at least as alert to relational niceties as Tractarians, Evangelicals, or scientific rationalists. Probably more so, because their cultural roots went deeper. George Eliot is a safer guide than Dickens here; and in so far as the chapels of those days *were* narrow and life-denying, and allowed the fine texture of Puritanism to be coarsened, not a little of the blame attaches to the Church of England for its consistent refusal either to treat Dissenters as human beings, or to share in the efforts being made to evangelize new and outwardly unpromising sections of the population.

But decency is no longer enough. Since the turn of the century, we have lived through a revolution in men's understanding of the motive forces behind human personality. Since Freud, whole generations have grown up which rightly perceive that there is more to their own and other people's behaviour than can be described solely in the old categories of right and wrong, sin and virtue; and their perception has created a whole new range of intellectual disciplines, together with new or revised techniques of social service and manipulation. It is not only the Free Churches which, with rare exceptions, have quailed from the task of assimilating all this

[1] A mental comparison of the world of Mrs Hutchinson's *Memoir* with the world of Restoration comedy makes the point.

into their understanding. The Church as a whole fell short, resenting the 'irreligion' of Freud as it resented the 'irreligion' of Darwin, and declining to criticize its concepts of sin and conscience, and the pastoral techniques which had grown out of these concepts.

This is not the place to discuss what this involves, but some of us have in our experience some atrocious instances of judgements passed by Dissenting clergy on people exhibiting symptoms of mental stress, and we are not confident that, even now, Free Church ministerial colleges equip men to take their place as pastors in a community where other professionally trained people are performing a similar or complementary function. Personally, I would never take any sort of problem to a clergyman unless I knew him very well first, simply because it is impossible to rely on finding the objectivity and elementary competence that the social sciences have given thousands of men and women outside the churches.

Certainly, no Christian would wish to say that 'sin' (for instance) is an outmoded concept, even though the word's debasement by theological illiterates has made it a difficult term for the popular imagination to grasp. But equally, Christians who work professionally in the field of mental disorder and family breakdown, however anxious they may be to find an accommodation between the Christian and the Freudian way of looking, find that the simple black-and-white categories which flow from Sunday School and pulpit are hard to work out and impossible to apply in this setting. Rather, they have to be unlearnt before professional progress can be made. When this has been done, they find themselves returning from the non-judgemental society of their weekday colleagues to seek the refreshment of worship among people still locked in the old dispensation—sincere indeed, but not by modern standards sensitive. Collectively and individually, modern Dissenting communities are very often, when one gets to know them, kind and generous both within and with-

out the fellowship. Rarely do they also give the impression
of being relaxed and understanding. They are not the sort of
places to which one could confidently recommend a dis-
charged prisoner, or a neurotic, or a divorcee. Often there is
an indefinable feeling of social—no doubt originally sexual—
tension, which shies away from self-knowledge and emotional
release, and hopes to erase from the inward feelings, or at
least from the outward behaviour, all the drives which pile
up for their possessors power, fortunes, prison sentences,
illegitimate children.

Clearly, this is most obvious in the nay-saying, lunatic
fringe of Nonconformity, where Moral Law Defence Associations are formed and a few rich, sanctimonious Tory MPs

'compound the sins they are inclined to
By damning those they have no mind to'.

But the same effect is discernible in much more moderate
form at the much less articulate level of the local chapel. As
yet, after all, no great body of opinion has arisen in the Free
Churches to tell the lunatic fringe plainly that its doctrines
are false and its pretensions intolerable. And only here and
there can one discern signs that the churches are starting to
catch up on the social skills of the last half century.[1]

It is because Dissenting chapels are what they are that the
failings I have been describing become apparent. The whole
burden of their theology and church order is towards
intimacy, the free exchange of personality and skills within
the fellowship. Far more than in the context of an Anglican
or Roman parish church, a person's deepest attitudes are
openly shared with others, not nursed in the secrecy of a

[1] See especially the excellent report on relationships between
the social services and the churches in a city suburb prepared
by the Birmingham Council of Churches in 1961; and the report
of Commission VII of the Congregational Union, recognizing
the claim of the statutory (as opposed to only the voluntary)
social services on Christian attention.

back pew. Of all the ecclesiastical institutions in Britain, the chapels can therefore least afford to lose the Puritans' 'sober concern for the evidence' and 'readiness to adapt to a changing world'. They also have the least excuse for losing these qualities, for Mr Hill, again, has written of 'the deeply theological connections between Puritanism and early science' in an essay on the covenant theology of John Preston:

> The service of mankind is the service of God: so conversely the achievements of mankind, the progressive discoveries of the arts and sciences, prove the existence of God, his care for his creatures... If the service of mankind is the service of a God who reveals himself in scientific and technical advance, many could support the Puritan cause who did not share Preston's own deeply personal religion. It was one of the many ways in which the greater rationalisms of the covenant theology broadened its appeal.[1]

This thread runs right through Dissenting history. One of the ejected ministers of 1662 was John Ray, the famous naturalist and classifier of plants. It was at the Protestant Dissenting Academies that the physical sciences, together with mathematics, geography and modern languages, first appeared in this country's educational curriculum; and, certainly, this is no time for Dissent's historic interest in scientific disciplines to be allowed to decline. As I suggest in the next chapter, a surprisingly high proportion of the new scientists and technologists are liable to come from a chapel background.

I have left to the last the first of all the qualities which Dr Green, in the passage I quoted on p. 47, attributes to the secular Puritan. This was 'a concern with right and wrong so keen as to set the tone of the whole personality'. (We may remember that even Bernard Manning's Lapsed Dissenter found his chapel upbringing 'sturdy, severe, morally bracing ...') The sub-Christian Puritan and the sub-Puritan Chris-

[1] *Op. cit.*, p. 273.

tian here march very close. The question is whether either
can survive. I quote here two passages which suggest fairly
strongly that they cannot. The first is a direct comment on
Dr Green's book, by David Marquand in *Encounter* for
September 1961 :

> Puritanism—even in the extended sense implied by Dr
> Green—rests on the two assumptions that moral absolutes
> exist, and that the individual human being can discover
> what these moral absolutes are and, by meditation on the
> word of God, gain the inner strength to regulate his life
> by them. Every intellectual advance from Darwin to
> Wittgenstein has made those assumptions more unten-
> able. Every recent discovery in the social sciences, from
> literary criticism to economics, has made it more obvious
> that the basis for morality must be social, not individual.
> It is true, no doubt, that the Puritan character structure
> has survived the destruction of the intellectual and moral
> foundations on which it was based. But it has survived
> as an empty shell, as a series of negative reflex actions no
> more coherent and logical than the gentleman-ideal itself.

The second passage is by Mr Hoggart, noting in a working class context the same profound change in public attitude,
expressed as a fondness for 'sincerity' as an end in itself :

> 'Well, at any rate 'e meant well, and that's all that
> matters' may become a cover for the lack of any confidence
> in the ability to reach a moral decision. . . . Thence flow
> wider evasions, an increasing use of phrases like 'After all,
> it's only natural', and 'Well, it does no one any harm',
> and 'It does y' good anyway, they say'. Or the evasions in
> language which make 'orthodoxy' and 'authority' auto-
> matically pejorative; and make gambling on the pools
> 'investments' : a history of the social importance of ideas
> could be traced in word changes like these. Everything is
> 'a matter of taste', and 'one man's meat is another man's
> poison'. . . .
> If this were carried forward, to meet a testing problem
> in ordinary life, the shock would be great; but in day-to-

day personal life earlier sanctions still to a great extent prevail. Yet no division like this can be healthy or more than temporary in the long run.[1]

Incidentally, the authors of both these passages themselves stand at one or two generations' remove from the chapels. The fate of the Free Churches is closely bound up with the changes described, both at the level of popular behaviour and at the level of intellectual argument. It is easy to recognize, in the relational rigidities of many chapelgoing people, the 'negative reflex actions' of a character structure which has survived the destruction of its intellectual and moral foundations. But equally, no one can go far in the Free Churches without lighting upon the new or newish cult of 'sincerity as an end in itself'—the first refuge of minds too lazy to rebuild their intellectual foundations—and the sentimental distrust of 'orthodoxy' and 'authority', in theological contexts at least.[2] Chapels are not immune from the climate of the time and place in which they are set: they absorb it as well as influence it. Mr Marquand has suggested to me in conversation that at two generations' remove from the chapel, a man still retains some of its attitudes and tone, but that when he has to think back to his great-grandparents to discover a Dissenting relative, the case is hopeless. I think he is right, and in this sense the climate in which the Free Churches have to work today is even now warmed by their

[1] *The Uses of Literacy* (Penguin ed. 1958) p. 195.
[2] To take a practical example: In England and Wales in 1952 nearly a fifth of all marriages taking place in Congregational churches and nearly an eighth of all taking place in Methodist churches were of divorced persons (as against 58 out of 173,282 in the Church of England). However true it may be that Anglican rules on divorce belong to law rather than grace, it is hard not to feel that many ministers are allowing their chapels to be extensively and blasphemously used as a social convenience by nominal Christians.

lost Edwardian glow. This warmth will not be available thirty
years on. Even now, 'morally bracing' is a term which one
would tend to apply to schools like Gordonstoun, or to the
prospectus of the Duke of Edinburgh's Award, rather than
to the typical chapel upbringing (though individual chapel-
going families may be able to supply what minister, Sunday
School and youth group cannot).

And yet ... and yet. The disappearance of the old
rigidities from the Free Churches is not a matter for regret.
If it did not happen we should become, like Christadelphians
or Jehovah's Witnesses, a sectarian irrelevance to the national
life. Moreover, we live in an age in which moral issues, as
opposed to the accepted vocabulary and contexts for discussing them, are alive precisely because the old rigidities are no
longer felt to be adequate. This is certainly true of sexual
morality; and the Aldermaston marches should have taught
us that it is still possible for political events and decisions to
affront the nonconformist consciences of people who have
little use for Nonconformity. And in a sense we are well rid
of the assumption 'that moral absolutes exist, and that the
individual human being can discover what these moral absolutes are and by meditation on the word of God, gain the
inner strength to regulate his life by them.' For it is not, *pace*
Mr Marquand, a Puritan assumption at all, but an assumption made by Nonconformity in the days of its decline. The
Puritans would be happy to agree that the basis for morality
is social, not individual. 'The Puritan preachers,' wrote Mr
Hill, 'attacked the individual conscience ... but they
thought, far more than their twentieth century successors,
in terms of the *Church*; a Church that was the nation,
society ...' The Puritans' meditation on the word of God was
thus public as well as private, and as their characteristic
phrase to announce the taking of a moral decision they used
(as the Quakers still do) 'It seemed good to the Holy Ghost
and to us', not 'In my quiet time this morning God told me
...' The individual element in Puritanism lay in the realm

of grace and salvation, in the person-to-person relationship of man to God, rather than in the interpretation of and adherence to a Kantian abstraction called the moral law.

Of course, no one would pretend that Puritanism, *tout court*, translates smoothly into the idioms of linguistic philosophy, the planned economy, and the Freudian ethic. Indeed, it is a strength of Puritanism that it is *an attitude to systems* rather than—like Thomism or Marxism—a self-contained system itself. I find it significant that it is this ideal towards which people of radical temper now seem to be groping. Dr Green is surely correct in thinking that the alternative ideal of 'the gentleman' (or 'Christian gentleman'), with which the Established Church is all too indelibly associated, is dead even while in *rigor mortis* it still grips our society. We may not accept Dr Green's characterization of George Orwell as a Puritan, but we may accept Orwell's description of England as 'a family with the wrong members in control'—a family where the important decisions are taken, not by the father and mother who have to bear the consequences, but by the quaint old grandparents, or an irresponsible bachelor uncle. It is an aspect of the Puritan ideal that it replaces connoisseurship with commitment, dilettantism with a sense of direction.

But there is a bandage over the eyes of those who are groping their way back to Puritanism, and only the Free Churches can unloose it. The Puritan type, as Mr Marquand points out even while rejecting it, is ultimately null and void without its Christian dimension, including an awakened conscience, an unsentimental awareness of human frailty, and an assurance of ultimate victory. Modern men are necessarily blind to this dimension, partly because they find Christian belief of any sort difficult, but partly because Puritan worship and culture and morality have been corrupted out of all recognition by the ecclesiastical bodies which claim to be the 'residuary legatees' of the tradition. This corruption is the real tragedy of 1662, and of the division in English life which followed: it is one of the reasons why so much hangs on the speedy attainment of reunion, and why so much generosity will be required—and justifiably required—of the Church of England on the road to it. Meanwhile, I have tried to suggest in this chapter that the Puritan tradition, properly understood, is still a live one; indeed, that it is the only fertilizing link between the Christian Church and society at large to which the Dissenting denominations still have exclusive access. Further to that, they possess a potential flexibility of organization and a much-advertised, though seldom seen, spiritual expansionism. It is enshrined in their mythology if not in their behaviour that the new way is probably better than the old way. When John Robinson took leave of the Pilgrim Fathers at Leyden in 1620, he told them (and the words are echoed in a hymn which many Dissenters are still fond of singing):

> I am verily persuaded the Lord has more Truth yet to break forth out of His holy Word. For my part, I cannot sufficiently bewail the Condition of the Reformed Churches, who are come to a Period in Religion and will go at present no farther than the instruments of their Reformation. The Lutheran can't be drawn to go beyond what Luther saw; and the Calvinists, you see, stick fast where they were left by that great man of God, who yet saw not all things.... I beseech you, remember, 'tis an Article of your Church Covenant, that you be ready to receive whatever Truth shall be made known to you from the written Word of God. . . .

Little though there may be left of the pilgrim mentality in the chapels today, the words are there and cannot be forgotten. They do not provide Dissent with a special objective of its own: the vision of a social order permeated with Christian values is no longer, if it ever was, ours alone. The routes to the objective are a different matter, and only Dissent is under quite this constitutional obligation to search out new routes, and when it is brought to a standstill—'a Period in

Religion'—to fan out and infiltrate new territories of human experience. Puritanism in all its aspects—ancient and modern, sacred and secular—leads straight on to what Tillich calls 'the courage to be'.

III

LEARNING: THE LOST IDEAL

The greatness of the Puritans is not so much that they con-
quered a wilderness, or that they carried a religion into it, but
that they carried a religion which was . . . indissolubly bound
up with an ideal of culture and learning. In contrast to all other
pioneers, they made no concessions to the forest, but in the midst
of frontier conditions, in the very throes of clearing the land and
erecting shelters, they maintained schools and a college, a stan-
dard of scholarship and competent writing, a class of men devoted
entirely to the life of the mind and of the soul.

Miller and Johnson, *The Puritans*, New York, 1938, p. 11.

EDUCATION is a huge and intimidating subject, not easily
reduced to order. So is Christianity. 'Christian education'
partakes of the difficulties set by both, the more so since all
good education asserts at least some Christian values, and all
good Christianity is essentially educative. Good education,
that is, looks at human beings singly, not as a mass, and
enables each of them to develop his or her talents and personality to the fullest, for private delight as well as for the
common good. This is a Christian concern too. Christianity,
on the other hand, is an education in itself: it teaches its
adherents how to live together in the Church under the discipline of mutual association and a common obedience, while
in its scriptures and its tradition it holds before them a great
literature and an absorbing history, both of which need creative interpretation by and for each fresh generation of
'students'.

It follows from all this that the concern of Christians with
education is many-fold. Even if the national religion taught

in Religious Knowledge periods were Confucianism or Mohammedanism—or Marxism—Christians would still be entitled, indeed obliged, to demand that the education provided in the other periods should be good, in the sense that I have described, because the interests of education itself here march with the emphases of Christianity. Equally, if people are to be taught Christianity, or taught about Christianity, at all, Christians have a duty to see that the teaching does justice to all its aspects, that knowledge of its aesthetic and historical glories is not imparted while knowledge of the living faith is neglected.

In an Educated Society

It is necessary to sketch in this philosophy of education as a strategic backcloth before analysing the tactical problem (or opportunity) which confronts any particular part of the Christian Church in a particular place at a particular time. It is well to be clear what we are trying to do. But the problem set for the Free Churches now by the direction which British education is taking does itself have a strategic aspect, for it raises another concern which Christians have with education. The Church does not only provide education from its own immense resources of subject matter, and sustain a critique of the education provided by others. Because Christianity is a historical religion, because Christians are ever charged with seeking the truth about the created world and the begotten Christ, the Church is singularly vulnerable to the advancement of knowledge. Part of what this vulnerability involves for her is the need to rearrange and adapt her temporal institutions, indeed her whole climate of thought, to the educational level reached by society at the material time. Such changes are always painful, and churchmen being what they are, there is usually a fierce internal battle to get these adaptations made soon enough; for example, to get the scriptures translated and competently interpreted in the vernacular before an emerging society has ceased to believe that the Church is bothered about its destiny. (This was the problem in Wyclif's England: in Asia and Africa it is the problem today.)

This chapter, then, chiefly discusses the relation of the Free Churches to the educational level reached by British society at this material time. Britain and America have been literate societies for centuries. But they are only now on the way to becoming 'educated societies', in which people can not only read—a skill useful even in a slave—but can develop their powers as free men, to the point where they will go on educating themselves all their lives. One arbitrary way of defining an educated society in numerical terms might be to say that it is a society in which a third of the total work force consists of college graduates. This will be the case in the USA in twenty years time. It would take this country about 150 years, at present rates of progress, to become an educated society on this criterion. But the rates of progress can, should, and in the end probably will be improved, and there is no doubt about the general direction in which we are moving. It is only a matter of time before even Tory Chancellors of the Exchequer accept Mr Peter Drucker's axiom that 'an abundant and increasing supply of highly educated people has become the absolute prerequisite of social and economic development in our world.'[1]

How these people are educated, and by whom, will obviously be a matter of concern at least to the thoughtful minority among denominational leaders. But the place of the Church in the coming society will not be dictated so much by Christian influence on teacher and curriculum, important as this is, still less by the teaching provided by the Church itself within her own circle, though this could be important if it were more competently done, as by the extent to which Christian institutions adapt to the sheer fact of the educated society by which they are surrounded.

[1] *Landmarks of Tomorrow* (Heinemann, 1959), pp. 114-117.

The novelty of the situation is obscured by several factors. In the first place, while great and increasing numbers of people in this country are being brought up without being exposed even to the elements of Christian history and theology, at least after their compulsory education is over, it is natural for the Church to assume that the problem it has to tackle is ignorance, not knowledge. But this is a mistake. It is easy to sigh that x per cent of grammar school pupils do not know what 'incarnation' means, that x per cent have illegitimate babies before they are sixteen, and that the populace at large finds it incomprehensibly difficult to distinguish the finer points of archiepiscopal thinking on the subject of divorce. All the same, there are a great many realms of modern knowledge and culture in which moderately intelligent young people today move more confidently than their senescent clerical critics, who often seem to hanker—no doubt unconsciously—after the not-so-distant days when ordination was a passport, sometimes even a short-cut, to membership of an educated élite, charged with keeping the light of sound learning alive in a rude, unlettered world.

This, indeed, is a second factor inhibiting adjustment to the modern world. The Church, whose clerks were once the main providers of education to the masses, still constitutes itself not unlike a rather stuffy regiment, where educated officer-clergy supervise moronic soldier-laity, instructing them in loyalty, regimental tradition and the customs of the depot, but never giving them a reason for an order. This is not how the New Testament envisages the soldiers of Christ. These resemble more precisely the members of a mountaineering expedition, who voluntarily grant the leadership to the man best equipped to find the route, plan the assault and encourage the faint-hearted; and who periodically set up camp to regroup and refresh themselves for the continuing struggle. Only in terms of an image like this is it possible to accept and welcome a development which leaves a significant proportion of the laity with more educational

skills than their vicar or pastor, intrinsically better able to
rationalize and manage much of the Church's business and
missionary outreach, local and national; yet possessing still
only an undeveloped spiritual capacity, often insensitive to
the direction which thought and planning must take if they
are to be of any ultimate use. And though it be objected that
for a long time to come the educational and cultural attainments of most church members will not be such as to make
possible the type of partnership that is envisaged, and though
it be further objected that even beyond congregations as they
are lie the unchurched and still very poorly schooled industrial masses, no advance whatever is possible until a beginning
is made in exploiting the resources now available. Certainly,
a reckless mortgaging of the Church's destiny to an 'educated'
minority, an ecclesiastical meritocracy, could leave us regret-
ting what we have (though it could not leave us much worse
off than we are *vis à vis* industrial workers). However, this
thesis looks to a time when the educated will be in a majority.
They cannot be prevented from forming their own characteristic secular institutions. But if the effort is made in time,
their institutions can at least be encouraged to reflect the
values of Christian churches.

The Response of the Churches

If we agree that there is a gauntlet to be picked up here,
what type of communion is equipped to answer the challenge? At first sight the Church of England seems worst off,
saddled as she is with a mediaeval-rural structure, ironclad
resistance to change, and manpower well into the sere and
yellow. In 1959, half the Church of England's working clergy
were over 50: that is, for the most part men who received
their formative education before 1920, usually in public
schools whose ideas were antediluvian even by the standards
of the time. And of the over-fifties, over a quarter were over
65, Victorians by birth and Edwardians by education.[1]

[1] *Facts and Figures about the Church of England* (CIO, 1961).

Some old men have much to give their flocks, simply by virtue of their age and experience. Some have the gift of perpetual youth. But one does not have to move far in the Church of England, especially in the country, to realize what a burden the age-curve of its clergy, allied to their traditional status and absolute authority, has by now become. Some of the Free Churches too have a ministerial age problem, but they are not gerontocracies on this scale.

However, are the Free Churches generally better placed to confront an educated society? I am not sure. They have assets, which are for the most part tucked under the bed in strong-boxes, and they also have liabilities. The latter first.

In the nineteenth century, and the early years of the twentieth, the Free Churches were organized, hardly less than the Church of England, to provide education. They did not have the Church of England's huge day school responsibilities, but they went very much further than the mere provision of Christian teachers to be fed into the emerging State system. Through their own Sunday schools and associated activities they provided not only an experience of religion but an introduction to a culture, and not for children primarily, but for adults. They were well aware why they did it. A Leeds Congregational minister, the Rev. R. W. Hamilton, defending the setting-up of Mechanics' Institutes at a time when the Established Church was still suspicious of them, put it like this:

> We cannot but place ourselves in firm resistance to the theory which urges, as a final cause of education, the mere preparation of men for particular positions in society. ... We say, Educate man as man, for what he is, for what he only can be, as accountable and immortal man.[1]

It was no accident that the Institutes in Leeds had at their inception a strong Unitarian, Congregational and Baptist flavour. But even more remarkable is the history of an insti-

[1] J. F. C. Harrison, *Learning and Living* 1790 – 1960 (Routledge, 1961), p. 176.

tution like Zion Sunday School, New Wortley, which was founded in 1832 by Wesleyan Methodists, aided by Quakers and Unitarians. On this school, Professor Harrison writes:

> From 1845 to 1867 it developed into what can perhaps best be described as a community centre. Its educational and social activities branched out into many directions far removed from its limited origins. Round the original Sunday School developed day schools for boys and girls (transferred to the School Board in 1871), evening classes, discussion groups, a mutual improvement society, a library (taken over by the local authority in 1870, thus becoming the first municipal library in Leeds), reading room, penny savings bank, dramatic groups, singing classes and choir, and annual school festivals with processions and banners. The New Wortley Mechanics' Institute and Youths' Guardian Society was formed at Zion, choir concerts in Leeds Town Hall originated from Zion, and it also pioneered the way in Leeds with cheap railway outings for the scholars, and (later) with Penny Readings.
>
> The potentialities of the Sunday School for the development of popular social and educational life could hardly be better illustrated than by this fertile institution. Beneath the omnibus title of the 'Zion Schools' lay a plethora of educational and social activities which cannot be wholly assessed in terms of the conventional institutional categories. Perhaps the greatest value of these activities as an adult educational force lay in the totality of the impact which they made upon the student.[1]

It is difficult today, surveying the mindless busy-ness, the jumble sales and ladies' sewing meetings, which now dominate the fringe activities of Dissenting communities, to recall that fifty years ago the chapels were a haven for those whom Raymond Williams has styled 'the socially and culturally under-privileged'. The downtown chapel literary society may not have been in the van of public taste, but neither did it straggle in the rear. It may not have had much time for

[1]*Op. cit.*, pp. 196-7.

aestheticism, but in this it probably both shaped and reflected the real values of most educated Victorians. Musically, too, the same can be said. One has only to read the music criticism of George Bernard Shaw, written in the eighties and nineties, and scan the programmes of Henry Wood's first Promenade Concerts, to realize that the music then acceptable to mass audiences was clearly related to the music habitually sung by chapel choirs. It is instructive to make the comparison with the present time, when quite ordinary young people can listen happily to the difficult (but often profoundly religious) output of Britten and Stravinsky, and all that the chapels will tolerate, at least in the north, is the gruesome twosome of Stainer's *Crucifixion* and Maunder's *Olivet to Calvary*.

Half a century has passed, and in that time the Free Churches, except perhaps in the remoter parts of Wales, have ceased to be a cultural source; they are like men standing by the bank down-stream, attempting to stain with religion a broadening river of secular culture which has risen in hills to which they have no access. It is rare now for people to go to chapel gatherings—I am not talking here about the Sunday services—to enrich their minds and imaginations, as men used to go to Silvester Horne's weeknight meetings at Whitefield's Tabernacle, or to the Adult Schools conducted on religious lines, usually by Quakers, for the pitifully-educated working class of the Edwardian era. Nowadays, the chapels are importers, not exporters, of cultural vitality. Their members acquire elsewhere—in schools and universities, from books and travel, even from the mass media—not only educational and vocational skills, but also their whole style of life.

A man is what he learns, and where he learns it. No institution, not even one whose primary *raison d'être* is the worship of God, can ultimately survive if it is unable to use, understand and assimilate the human powers of its members at the point of development they have reached; for on this use, understanding and assimilation depend the content and the wholeheartedness of the worship that is offered. I venture the suggestion that there are few well-educated Free Churchmen under the age of forty who are not, as it were, holding something back as they share in church life—something, no matter what, which their education has given them and which they dare not communicate to the brethren and so offer to God for fear that it will be rejected or misunderstood.

This, of course, goes far deeper than the mere loss by Dissent of a function once performed in the field of popular education. But it may perhaps be opined that the loss of this function to the State, welcome and necessary though this development was, had something to do with the subsequent cooling in the Free Churches of the Puritan spirit of inquiry into matters other than strictly religious, and with the decline in the intellectual rigour which was applied to religious matters too.[1] Those who no longer had to dispense education to others no longer looked for it themselves. . . . The decline has not been uniform, for it is a matter of common observation that the Free Churches have contributed at least their fair share of first-rate Biblical scholars and theologians to the Church in recent generations. But this is not quite the point. It is more pertinent to inquire how far such men are honoured in the farthest corners of their denominations for what they write and think, rather than for the prestige they confer; and how far the prevailing anti-intellectual climate of the churches, including many of the most prosperous, limits the exercise and appreciation of their talents to universities and ecumenical conversations.

There has in fact developed within the Free Churches during the twentieth century a divorce between learning and administration which has gone much farther than in the Church of England, and which is completely foreign to the

[1] Dr Martin Green, writing about *The Sunday Times* (Op. cit., p. 32) shrewdly observes: 'The religious piece is obviously written for a much less alert mind than Atticus or George Schwartz or E. H. Brooks & Son.'

tradition, possessed by Orthodox Dissent at least, of a 'learned ministry'. The writer of the prefaces to *Crockford* is always complaining about the steady deterioration in the academic attainments of Anglican bishops, and up to a point it can be objected against him that we live in the heyday of the specialist and that in a time of shortage it is a waste of resources to turn good scholars into bad bureaucrats. However, never was the Church more in need of theologically alert administrators.

Of course, at the institutional level, shortcomings have been exceedingly hard to avoid. Congregationalists, for instance, have only recently come to accept a moderatorial system and a strong central administration. They have not yet awarded the occupants of these advisory/supervisory positions the respect and conditions of work commensurate with the demands made on them, and it is surprising that the demands are in fact so often met. But at local level too it is by no means uncommon to find the things of the mind treated either with damaging neglect or ill-concealed scorn. It is rare indeed to find an adequate bookstall in a chapel, and almost as rare to hear a contemporary book or journal, religious or secular, recommended from the pulpit. This would have puzzled the Puritans and greatly distressed our great-grandfathers; nor can it entirely be ascribed to the preponderance within our churches of elderly and middle-aged women. It may even be partially responsible for this preponderance.

Another grave problem for the Free Churches is the social mobility which is inseparable from educational advance. Bernard Manning's irreverent treatment of this topic should not be allowed to obscure its fundamental seriousness. In America, where sociological studies are not despised by religious leaders, there is less temptation to overlook how group shifts of income, employment, education and residential district can damage beyond repair religious institutions whose character was shaped in the past by a different set of social forces. Every year we mourn—or more often, shrug off—

our 'lapsed Dissenters'. Less often do we inquire rigorously and self-critically into the reasons why these people have, in the picturesque Methodist phrase, 'ceased to meet'. We content ourselves with facile references to the faithlessness of the times and the neglect of some church officers. Less superficial inquiry is needed on all fronts, but I am here concerned with a single category of the lapsed. Why, when a Free Church minister speculates on the future of his flourishing little youth group, can he tell himself that the members most likely to be Anglicans or nothing at all by the time they are twenty-five are the ones who go away to college or university, Oxbridge especially?

I hope it will by now be clear that I do not personally regard a Dissenter's 'lapse' into Anglicanism as something to be sneered at—quite the contrary. I am not disturbed because people switch from Chapel to Church for bad reasons: I am disturbed because the reasons are generally so good. It may be true that 'no man by taking thought can become an Anglican'. I doubt if it is true these days that many Free Churchmen, at least the highly-educated ones, become Anglicans without taking thought at all (unless their membership of both communions was and remains entirely nominal). But what may be an individual's salvation, and a profit to the 'receiving' communion, is the 'giving' communion's crippling loss. It was an elderly Methodist minister of strong ecumenical convictions who lamented to me last year that it was the young people his denomination could least afford to lose who were being confirmed in the Church of England, and he ran through a striking list of recent ex-presidents of the Methodist Conference whose sons and daughters were Methodists no longer. This man thought that in nearly all cases the 'corybantic formlessness' of much Methodist worship was the prime cause for the flight of the educated from Methodism, and I am sure that similar dissatisfactions account for the similar flight from all Nonconformist denominations, including those whose worship could be more accurately described as pedestrian than as corybantic.

But there are less explored social causes too. Graduates, it should be remembered, virtually never return after their university careers to the churches which produced them. Only seldom do they return to the same type of church in the same type of locality. The first-generation graduate brought up in a Welsh mining valley or a Lancashire mill town—a faithful Sunday School pupil, perhaps even already a church member —becomes an advertising executive in St John's Wood or an industrial chemist in a Cheshire dormitory suburb. Behind him, if he has retained his Christian convictions, lie the inter-denominational experiences of the university. Even if he has remained wrapped in his own denomination's society while at college, in the outside world he is as likely to be struck by the contrast as by the affinity between this type of fellowship and the churches of his faith and order as they actually are. And for the first time in his life he and his wife are free, entirely free to choose the community to which they will give their Christian allegiance, without the pull of family tradition to affect their own judgement of what is best for them. In many districts, the parish church is the only possible choice.

There are naturally very few graduates indeed who are travelling in the reverse direction geographically. As a result, the chapels of the industrial north and rural west have no fresh source of vitality to draw on.[1] They may even lose their sense of belonging to the same enterprise as the flourishing new chapels which do now exist (for the benefit of their migratory children) in many metropolitan dormitory suburbs. Yet even in their dying spasms the declining Zions and Ebenezers of the dales and the valleys are capable of

[1] Unless they can draw on the Pentecostalist and 'enthusiastic' sects on their ecclesiastical Left. This form of progression has been little explored sociologically. But there is also movement the other way, notably from nominal Anglicanism and Dissent into exotic sects – the Mormons, in particular.

begetting yet another wave of young people intelligent enough to be snatched away by the next wave of educational expansion—and these in their turn are likely, on present trends, to feel even more loosely attached to their denomination and to Dissent as a whole.

The Assets of the Free Churches

Not all the tensions in the Free Churches just now are caused by the innate conservatism of all ecclesiastical institutions in the face of unprecedented challenges. Difficulties are inevitably caused by the projection into church life of the social cleavages and inequalities which bedevil our whole educational system. Just as old-established policemen object to suggestions that graduates might go straight into the higher reaches of the Force without the preliminary years on the beat, old-established chapelgoers look askance at the pretensions of the educated, whom they accuse, not without some justice, of striking attitudes, complicating simple issues, shirking the hard work of running bazaars, and forgetting that intellectual attainment is not uniquely pleasing to God. While the 'away-educated' were a tiny minority among Free Church young people this type of reaction could hardly be avoided, though quantitatively the problem has remained too small to be much noticed. In the future, at least if some means can be found of arresting their flight from the chapels, such people will no longer be in such a small minority, and out of the tension good may come. In other words, the Free Churches themselves will become 'educated societies' long before the country as a whole becomes so, and they would do well to recognize the fact instead of looking wistfully after the industrial workers (whom they seldom had in their pews anyway, outside Wales). Already the rapid expansion of Free Church denominational societies in universities has demonstrated that the *nouvelle vogue* of students includes very many from chapel backgrounds. This was to be expected, and will continue, for chapelgoers on the whole exhibit exactly those qualities and sociological characteristics which make them likely parents of first-generation graduates as universities reach further and further down the social bran-tub for their student intake.[1] Chapelgoers (as we have noted) number among their ranks very few unskilled manual workers and comparatively few artisans, but they include a great many clerical and minor administrative workers, professional men and businessmen. These classes have a highly developed sense of responsibility towards their children, and if their children are selected by the State for higher education, these are not the sort of parents to say no. Thirty years ago, it would have been a difficult or impossible proposition financially for many of them, but now this is not so.

These changes have had a visible effect on most universities but most of all on Oxford and Cambridge, where before the war the dominant ethos, where it was Christian at all, was predominantly Anglican. It still is, but the balance is shifting, at least in the undergraduate body. In adapting to the educated society, and in building on the close-knit relationship between education and Christianity sketched at the beginning of this chapter, the Free Churches have this advantage: for the first time since the Ejectment 'their people' will be in the mainstream of British secular education, depending almost wholly upon it for all that they know, becoming critical users and perhaps supervisors.

Assuming, as I do throughout this book, that the Free Churches as institutions (not just the individuals who belong to them) have at their best a very great deal to offer contemporary society, it is hard to overstate the importance of this. It means that they have over the next twenty-odd years a strictly non-recurring chance of coming back from the margin to somewhere near the centre of national life, and

[1] University Populations

University Populations	1938/9	1948/9	1958/9	1968/9 (Government
	50,000	80,000	100,000	175,000 permitting)

incidentally of shaking off the cultural inferiority complex which the misinterpreters of Puritanism have so successfully brainwashed into them. But clearly this opportunity depends wholly on the Free Churches' managing to keep the loyalty of their educated sons and daughters, whose contribution is likely to be proportionate to the intellectual and spiritual demands made on them.

A further advantage possessed by the Free Churches in the era of the educated society is that they are (or ought to be) in favour of it. When earlier in this chapter I caricatured the Church as 'a rather stuffy regiment' Dissenting readers, however reformist, will have shaken their heads, saying that they have not so learned Christ. Though I hope to show that not even Dissent is nowadays exempt from the ecclesiastical equivalent to messroom taboos, on the whole they are right. The Puritan attitude to the interpretation of Scripture, and the Puritan tradition of preaching from William Perkins to Robert Dale, not only favour an educated society, they presuppose it. So do the Presbyterian and Congregational/ Baptist methods of church government. They presuppose, that is, not an educated technological society in the modern sense (for Christians, who have often learnt to read with the single object of being able to read the Bible, have not often learnt the Second Law of Thermodynamics with equal disregard for worldly advantage); but at least a community of literate, inquiring people. The world-wide pressures towards education today may be economic and political rather than theological, but we have seen that people of the Puritan sort did not stick at mere Biblical literacy and political quietism; and we have seen how, from the founding of the Dissenting Academies to the founding of London University, they coveted the best learning for themselves, even though—or perhaps because—history had put them at a heavy social and cultural disadvantage. And although the intellectual demands made by most chapels on their members are nowadays kept to a minimum, education as such (to be distinguished from behaving like an educated person) is still thought of in these societies as an unmixed good.

The maliciously inclined may like to suggest that this is because of the economic status it confers: chapel people, like the rest of society in the 1960s, see 'a good post' within the reach of their children, and react accordingly. But at least in chapelgoers' attitudes towards the educational explosion there is very little of the ambivalence, the fundamental scepticism, which affects the upper reaches of English society (I purposely do not include Scottish society here). Nor, from their different standpoints, do either Roman Catholics or Anglicans in this country quite share Dissent's acceptance of education as an unmixed good for all, even though Rome and Canterbury as institutions make much more determined efforts than the Free Churches to secure for their children the schooling which they find compatible with their beliefs. Anglicanism, for example, does not by its own nature and form of government demand an educated society within itself, and hence not in the community at large either. At least until very recently, it has been content with an educated élite. (The more credit, of course, to the Church of England at the present time for initiating so many small but fruitful experiments in educational fields which should have been more faithfully cultivated by the Free Churches.) And in so far as the typical Anglican is still a Tory voter, his subconscious doubt about the need to educate the masses is at the present time reflected in the country's political priorities.[1]

---

[1] There have been few detailed studies of denominational voting habits. But A. H. Birch in his study of Glossop *Small Town Politics* (Oxford, 1959) showed how industrial workers with a religious allegiance voted there in the 1951 General Election. Of the active Anglicans, 55 p.c. voted Conservative, 5 p.c. Liberal and 29 p.c. Labour. Of the Nonconformists, 25 p.c. voted Conservative, 16 p.c. Liberal and 44 p.c. Labour. It must be emphasized that these were industrial workers.

Dissenters in Education

In this chapter so far I have been examining the Free Church future in an educated society on a rather narrow front—though a front which has perhaps seen too little campaigning. On this front the reasons for optimism scarcely balance the reasons for pessimism. It is at least painfully clear that if the Free Churches continue over the next twenty years to lose young educated people from their ranks, not merely at the rate they are losing them now but several times faster because of the leap forward in higher education, they are doomed in their present form. Now that the big battalions have melted away from the pews, the chapels depend very heavily on their highly educated minority for the ministry and leadership which is capable of adapting their institutions to the modern world. It is hard to see how all the forms of renewal—Biblical, sacramental, theological, liturgical—which are now discernible in some places, can become generalized throughout the denominations quickly enough to 'revive our drooping churches' in places where many have already drooped—on worldly calculation—below the point of no return. At least, it will be a close-run thing.

I have, of course, been discussing only one of the social habits through which one particular social group is probing the shortcomings of the Church's present institutional structure. I have presented it as a problem of 'lapsed Dissenters' who must needs be retained, or recovered, if Dissent is to keep any power at all to shape its own role in the future, but there would be no point in bothering about this problem at all unless the future role envisaged is itself to be a missionary one; unless, that is, the salvaged 'backsliders' are to be used as a nucleus of new religious institutions in which their hitherto alienated and secularized contemporaries may also one day find a home. This has nothing to do with any wistful schemes which may here and there be envisaged for building up the Free Churches to their pristine magnificence. Rather, it is a matter of using Dissenting attitudes, insights, social and intellectual capital to help Christianity to keep pace with a period of rapid social change.

It is not part of my intention to offer a blueprint for Free Church educational activity in the type of society now emerging in Britain. Nevertheless, I shall suggest one or two lines of exploration in the light of the relationship between Christianity and education which I assumed at the outset of this chapter. Dissenters do have fruitful contributions to make, both to the general secular debate about education in Britain today, and to any reappraisal undertaken of the Church's own educational aims and resources.

But before even this brief discussion begins there is a bogy to be laid. Teachers, politicians and churchmen, their ears still ringing with the din of battles not-so-long-ago, are apt to suppose that Dissenters' concern with education begins and ends with opposition to ecclesiastical control of State financed schools. For a century this was the main political issue between Dissent and its ecclesiastical opponents. Yet all through the nineteenth century, there was a sense in which education itself was never the issue at all. It was merely the occasion. The truculent Nonconformists of 1902, who went to prison rather than comply with the Education Act which put 'Rome and Canterbury on the rates', were interested not so much in how children were educated, as in by whom. The same went for other Christian traditions in this period, though there were naturally individuals whose concern went much deeper. One recalls that the classical statement of the principles which should govern university education was enunciated by John Henry, later Cardinal, Newman.[1]

---

[1] *The Idea of a University.* Newman's religion was certainly bound up with an ideal of culture and learning. There was also something of the Puritan in him, with his exaltation of conscience, his susceptibility to conversion experiences, and his sensitivity to human personality. This was perhaps the secret of his hold over those of his contemporaries who least agreed with him ecclesiastically.

It would be a great mistake to project the sterilities of the education controversy into future decades. Despite the brief flare-up in 1959, when the Government increased the main-tenance grants to church schools from 50 per cent to 75 per cent and included new secondary schools in the bargain, there is now in the Free Churches a general, if unspoken, feeling that even if 'our folk' were wholly in the right on this matter—a debatable proposition—we would have nothing to gain, and inter-church relations in Britain would have a great deal to lose, if we maintained a pernickety insistence on 'our rights'.[1] With the Established Church, indeed, peace has been cemented, at least at the national level, and many Free Church parents these days are only too happy to send their children to an Anglican primary school if they can find a good one. In today's altering climate, even the fear of Roman Catholic aggrandizement may fade. Sociologically and ecumenically, it is indeed a great pity that Roman Catholic children are educated without being exposed to that en-counter with children of different religious backgrounds which many of us value in our own upbringing; and if the Hierarchy were ever to extend its demands for 'separate development' into the universities—proposing, for example, separate, subsidized halls of residence—a new stand would

[1] Principal John Huxtable in his 1961 Cadoux Lecture, *Church and State in Education* (Religious Education Press) observed that a great number of Free Churchmen now embraced the Anglican conviction that church and school belong together, and were dis-satisfied with what their fathers did in 1870 and 1902. 'The gulf between what the Free Church experts in education desire, and what the guardians of Free Church tradition declare is danger-ously wide'. The hostile reception this got in the *Baptist Times* merely proved his point. Surely we can now admit to ourselves that our forefathers' over-riding mistake was to deny their own churchmanship, as well as that of their opponents. Reacting against Anglican arrogance, they appeared to claim that 'The Bible' and 'non-sectarian religion' in a school curriculum amounted to a Christian education. But of course, they do not.

have to be made.[1] But for the moment, what chiefly matters to Free Churchmen as taxpayers is that Roman Catholic children should not be at an educational disadvantage. The demand for separateness should entail some additional burden on the communion which makes it, but not a disproportionate one. As taxpayers, we are still educating Roman Catholic citizens on the cheap.

By the outbreak of the 1939-45 War, the long debate on the politics of education in Britain had sapped most Nonconformists' desire to think about its content. While the 1944 Education Act was being prepared, a contributor to the *British Weekly* began an article on 'Worship in Schools' by apologizing for bothering his readers with a subject 'which seems at first sight to belong only to the limited field of education'. But this Act, which put the onus on churches and local authorities to agree syllabuses for an entirely new system of State-provided religious education, did begin to convert many Free Churchmen from a negative vigilance to a more positive concern with the opportunities for Christian education now available outside the domestic circle of Sunday school and youth group. The inter-dependence of all that a child learns, from whatever source, impressed itself at least on the leaders of Christian opinion. And although 'R.I.' as actually provided in many schools is ludicrously bad—not so much a foretaste of the faith as an inoculation against it—in others it is much better than that, and the syllabuses of several local authorities make it quite clear that religious instruction in schools is meant to lead to church membership. There are even a few straws of evidence that it may actually do so. A recent survey of Ilford schoolchildren suggested that the proportion of *grammar school* pupils admitting allegiance

[1] Bishop Beck of Salford has recently been appealing for funds to build university hostels for Catholic Students. On the other hand, the activities of Opus Dei, which include the financing of such hostels, are in disfavour with many English Roman Catholics.

to church and chapel has risen from 36 per cent to 51 per cent in the past twelve years. Such evidence should be treated cautiously, since other influences (SCM in Schools, for example) have been at work, and anyway, the children who first went to primary school on the day the 1944 Act came into force are now only just emerging into adulthood. It is probably far too early to calculate the Act's effect on the religious health of the nation, beyond observing that the verdict, when it is made, will not necessarily confirm the unflattering mental stereotype of post-war youth which most people cherish.

In fact, it is very questionable whether there now is, could be, or should be, a distinctive Dissenting viewpoint on education as such. It is one of the many fields where it is the first duty of Free Church leaders and spokesmen, local and national, to concert their strategy with their counterparts in other denominations—even other religions—and with the teaching profession itself. This will involve adding their voices, at full lung-power, to the demand for more and better education, and the taxes to pay for it. Then, in resisting as Christians the impersonality inherent in an urban society where men's lives are disposed more by technology than by personal choice, they will recall that it is often only the schoolchild who lives and works in the same community, that the school presents to a child and through him to his parents a unique and non-recurring chance of achieving a responsible personal life in 'given' community. At this point Dissenters will begin to realize the potentialities latent in the 'church schools' which their ancestors fought for so long, and they might be willing to explore the interesting suggestion of State-aided, interdenominational primary schools, to be started as centres of community healing in a few areas of upward social mobility.[1] If such an experiment were

[1] Daniel Jenkins, *Equality and Excellence* (SCM Press, 1961), p. 130.

launched—or even if it were not—they would soon begin to share the concern of Dr Cunliffe-Jones 'to relate the community of the school to the different social situations and groupings manifestly lacking in community, into which those educated will go.'[1]

As far as the actual religious instruction given in State schools is concerned, an approach concerted among all the churches in a particular area can do much to discourage local authorities, and head teachers, from trying to teach the faith simply as a history or a literature. But above all Dissenters need to remember, both as parents and as church members, that (as Professor Niblett puts it)

> Christian education is not only, perhaps not even chiefly, a matter of teaching religious knowledge or the text of the Bible. The way in which science, literature, history are taught has a great and unavoidable bearing on our pupils' understanding of things. . . . To put a scientific or literary education inside a Christian framework is to do in the life and upbringing of the individual what history has been doing for a thousand years in the life and growth of western society. . . . It is clear enough that one of the main needs if children are to be educated with a Christian outlook is a supply of teachers of many subjects other than religious knowledge, as well as divinity itself, who understand the importance of their own presuppositions.[2]

This type of concern—to see that 'science, literature, history' are taught in a way which permits a Christian understanding of them—is precisely what used to be central to the outlook of almost all educated Free Churchmen, whether professionally concerned with schools or not, and what is

[1] *Technology, Community and Church* (Independent Press, 1961), p. 116.
[2] *Christian Education in a Secular Society* (Oxford, 1960), pp. 123, 126.

now virtually confined to teachers among Dissenters. Partly, this is due to the pietistic segregation of religion from life which has already been noticed as a kind of wet-rot in once sturdy Puritan timbers. Partly, it may be due to Dissenters lack of experience and direct personal concern in running schools themselves. Indeed, the few Free Church fee-paying institutions which survive reflect all too faithfully the stresses—material, intellectual and sociological—under which the Free Churches themselves have laboured in this century. The Quaker public schools appear to have been the most successful in retaining the distinctive style of their associated religious body. Several of the others have degenerated into something hard to distinguish in ethos from the typical, lukewarmly Anglican minor public school, and their conception of a Christian education is not any richer or more whole-hearted than a good grammar school's. This, in turn, is surely because the Free Church schools no longer draw a high proportion of their pupils from the solid Dissenting families which were once to be found in the land, but from the children of the great army of newly prosperous, 'undenominational' Christians who, if they were themselves brought up in chapels, were not taught there to associate religion with an ideal of culture and learning. The reservation of a few places at these schools for the children of Dissenting clergymen and missionaries has not—how could it have been?—enough to arrest this degeneration.

Children in Church

It is the lack of a general sense that education is indivisible which hamstrings much of the educational provision traditionally made by churches on Sundays for children of school age. True, there has been a little belated self-criticism here. One is even able to cite a recent study commissioned by the Free Church Federal Council (not a notably self-critical body) for the conclusion that Christian education in Britain today is in 'a muddle'.[1] The interdenominational committee responsible for this study reported that in day schools, Sunday Schools, Girl Guides, youth clubs and children's addresses different material was being presented by people with patently different attitudes to the Bible; and that young people were being given their Christian education (understood by this group in a narrower sense than Professor Niblett's), not only by different instructors, but by different instructors working to diverse programmes, with diverse standards, from diverse points of view, and with diverse aims.

It is not surprising (though it may be a comment on the tragic lack of co-operation between the local churches and the day schools) that in several areas school leavers' religious clubs are springing up to meet the continuing need of those who first found love and guidance in the religious instruction lessons of their day schools.

It would certainly not be surprising if children exposed to this degree of pedagogic confusion fled into fundamentalist funk-holes at the earliest opportunity. The committee lays the blame for the situation fairly and squarely on the disunity of the churches, 'which almost entirely prevents the creation of those intimate informal links between the schools and the local churches which would enable the child to move easily from school to the church. . . . Any approach to the county day school is strengthened if it is an approach of all the local churches together; in fact it may be doubted whether a county day school ought to respond to an offer of co-operation from only one denomination.'

In some areas, of course, not only the integration of school and Sunday school, but even the integration of Sunday school and church, is a new idea. In this connection, a Lancashire vicar once remarked to me that when he came to the county he 'naively imagined' that Sunday school meant the

[1] *Church, Child and School* (FCFC, 1960). And see *Growing Christians* (British Council of Churches, 1957).

instruction of children in the faith. But he soon learnt that in many localities the school preceded the church historically, and had grown up and survived as a social entity on its own, of the type described by Professor Harrison in the passage from which I quoted earlier in this chapter. Many of the vicar's Dissenting colleagues could describe similar survivals from vanished situations.

Taking all these factors into account, together with the changing English use of Sunday, it is hardly surprising that there are now less than half the children in Free Church Sunday Schools than there were in 1900 (though even so, there are still well over a million). It is more surprising, perhaps, that the decline has not been uniform. Churches on housing estates, and churches which have adopted the 'family church' system devised by the Congregationalists during the 1930s, still often find that the numbers of children exceed the supply of space and teachers. Indeed, perhaps it is this last 'success' which has made it seem in rather bad taste to question whether Sunday schools as a whole can reasonably be expected to discharge what they would presumably regard as their primary task: the building up of boys and girls into Christian men and women. Free Churchmen, and most Anglicans, assume that Sunday schools (by whatever name) are important, and that the time and energy necessarily absorbed by them is well spent.

It is not my purpose directly to contradict this assumption, dogmatically asserting that Sunday schools have served their day and should be abolished. There is simply not enough evidence to come to such a hard and fast conclusion. But we may reasonably regret that the considerable improvements which have been wrought since the Butler Act, in the details of Sunday school organization and curriculum, were not accompanied, or better still preceded, by more radical probing, into the limitations inherent in the whole system. It is true that the quality, and hence the usefulness, of the Sunday schools we have vary enormously in different situations, and it would be absurd to 'kill' organizations successfully meeting a felt local need. But the inherent limitations make it possible to suggest that the energy—and funds—lavished on the more moribund Nonconformist Sunday schools in their present form is quite out of proportion to the effect. Indeed, there are many schools which—from the greenery-yallery Jesus-posters on the walls to the antiquated Biblical knowledge of the superintendent—do much more harm than good.

The chief practical limitation was imposed when the 1944 Act laid down that all children should receive religious instruction in their day schools. This shifted at a stroke the Church's main educational responsibility from children to older teenagers and to adults. At least in theory, churches no longer needed to teach young children what the faith is and what the Bible is about; but only to give them the practical experience of worship and a Christian community's life. Clearly, more than this often had to be done in practice, but this was —and is—the intention.

The danger in the new system was that school-leavers, even those who were the children of churchgoing parents, would put away the Christian faith with other childish things. The first task of the Church became the making of the faith visibly relevant in the world beyond age fifteen, on the shopfloors of factories and in the sixth forms of grammar schools.[1] This was a task for which very few local churches, let alone local Free churches, were equipped in the 1940s and 1950s. Urgent re-tooling was called for. This was the more necessary since in people over fifteen, churches no longer have a captive audience of children who will often come to church whether their parents are members or not, but a wayward group of adolescents undergoing rapid secularization in their work and leisure, and sometimes in their further education too. The Church in its educative capacity is often unable to approach this group—and for that matter all adults—direct. It can

[1] See C. F. Wild's pamphlet *From School to Work* (National Society, 1962).

only hope to raise up teachers and lay apostles from its own membership, and look to them to take their own mature understanding of Christianity into a workaday world which is happy to associate Christianity with childish things.

The practical consequence of this reversal, in a typical church on an ordinary Sunday morning, might well have been the reversal of habits which have become sacrosanct simply because time-honoured. Instead of the children 'study-ing' while the adults worshipped, perhaps it should have been the adults who studied while the children worshipped. Sup-pose a local situation where the religious instruction in day schools is being well done, to a good syllabus, by (for the most part) competent and Christian teachers.

This is perhaps more likely to be the case in the type of area where chapels nowadays flourish, and in the type of secondary school which chapelgoers' children are most likely to attend. The church's task is to supplement what a child is already receiving from his home and his school. The sup-plement needed will be education in actual membership of a worshipping, responsible community. Any attempt, especi-ally an amateurish attempt, to teach the child religious know-ledge—say, Bible stories and lives of Dissenting saints—is in some danger of confusing him, unless the co-ordination be-tween school, church and home is far better than it is in most localities. But worship is an art, which can only be taught by participation, at the nearest to adult level which a child of a particular age can manage. A church which was taking its 'supplementation' task seriously might hand the whole of its Sunday morning service over to its children, with their parents and supervisors, to work out their own liturgy, under ministerial guidance in the first instance. (Such liturgies would need to follow the historic liturgies of the Church closely in pattern, though not necessarily in content.) Scep-tics should pay a visit to the Sunday services of the Dragon School, Oxford—a boys' preparatory school—to be reminded of the lengths to which it is possible to go in handing the conduct of worship over to children, when the children are carefully trained and a tradition has been established.

Meanwhile, the adults of the church would be presented with several alternative diets of Christian observance on a Sunday. They could attend the main service of public worship, in the evening.[1] They could support the children's morning service. But in the mornings they would be encouraged to form themselves into groups for studying the Bible, best of all in each other's homes, each group celebrating its own communion service together from time to time. (The main communion services of the whole church could form part of the liturgy for Sunday evening.) Since God has given us a flexible liturgy, let us enjoy it.

The other limitations inherent in Sunday schools at the present time must be briefly passed over. Most local churches simply lack the manpower and womanpower to do a decent job. While the churches themselves are so weak, their Sunday schools can never be much more than creches—a praiseworthy gesture of friendship to the neighbourhood, but in themselves no substitute for the religious education of home and school, and only a temporarily effective net for drawing 'stranger' children within the orbit of the church. Those who teach in such Sunday schools, which are unfortunately often set in localities where religious instruction in State schools is itself vestigial, are often in need of Christian education as badly as their pupils—and shall babes lead the babes?

It follows that Sunday schools, except for a few of the most professionally conducted ones, are not any longer an obvious direct means of gathering into the household of God young people who would not otherwise be there. Even if a particular church is lucky enough to have within its membership a group of professional teachers, it is at least debatable whether it should expect them to spend their weekends, not

---

[1] Obviously this suggested pattern is an alternative, not an adjunct, to the pattern passingly noticed in Chapter I.

in ridding themselves of their occupational neuroses and re-charging their spiritual and intellectual batteries, but in activities which mirror their weekday jobs and often make it difficult for them to participate fully in the worshipping life of the church. For unfortunately, it is all too often the case today that a church's Sunday School teachers are its least mature members.

The evangelical energy (not to mention the financial and administrative resources) which the Free Churches have in the past devoted to their Sunday schools should be largely diverted to the new growing points of Christian education in our society; points, moreover, where much less help can be expected from the State. At local level this means, for in-stance, straining every nerve to establish efficiently-run, properly-housed 'open' youth clubs, no less than home-based Bible study groups working with up-to-date interpretative material. Nationally and regionally, it means something much better than the lukewarm permissiveness which is still the commonest Dissenting attitude to specialized chaplain-cies (in youth work, higher education, industry). The Church of England has recently been making the Free Churches look very silly in this respect by its charting of new ways for seeking the people where they may be found.

IV

CLERICALISM—CHAPEL STYLE

The introverted church is one which puts its own survival
before its mission, its own identity above its task, its internal
concerns before its apostolate, its rituals before its ministry. . . .
Undue emphasis on the static structure of the Church has led to
the disappearance of a signficant lay ministry in denominational
Protestantism. . . . The more introverted the Church, the more
it becomes subject to priestcraft.

Gibson Winter, *The Suburban Captivity of the Churches*
(SCM Press, 1961), p. 103.

DR WINTER is an American, and his critique of the 'organization Church', preening itself in metropolitan suburbs, belongs in the first place to the American religious scene. As
such, it may be thought to have but little relevance to the
condition of the Free Churches in Britain today. American
church life seems to us to be in one sense years ahead and in
another sense years behind our own. The religious boom in
the United States today has certain resemblances to the one
which overtook Britain in the Victorian era. On the other
hand the context of social life in the States, from which the
churches take their protective colouring, is generally assumed
to represent the blissful or dreadful prospect which for the
British is still thirty years or so in the future. Organization
Man has only recently landed in this country, and he is only
beginning to set about making Organization Church in his
own image. There are other important differences between
churches there and here: for instance, we are not yet riven
with dissension over the problem of admitting negroes to
membership of our Christian institutions.

But there are similarities too, and some of our problems may be clarified in the methodical studies which the American religious phenomenon has evoked. There is certainly something to be learnt from Dr Winter's comment that the 'introverted' church is a breeding-ground for priestcraft, however averse, in theory, its members are from clerical dominance. Several theologians on this side of the Atlantic have made the same point. Dr E. L. Mascall has written of 'the clericalism of the Word which is every bit as radical (and, we might add, as unprimitive) as any clericalism of the sacraments had ever been in Catholicism'.[1] To this Anglo-Catholic opinion Daniel Jenkins has added a Dissenting one:[2]

> No matter what their official theology may be, the situation of ministers in relation to their churches is such that it can seem the most natural thing in the world to proceed on the assumption that the primary function of churches as institutions is to maintain their ministers, not only in the financial sense but in the more pervasive sense of providing a milieu in which ministers can freely exercise their gifts.

Priestcraft, in fact, is fostered whenever and wherever the *laos*, the whole people of God, begins to view the ordained ministry as an office rather than as a function, and allows the office to shape the function rather than the function to shape the office. Most churches and most Christians in Britain—the denomination is immaterial—conceive the ministry as a professionalized caste with its own exclusive tabus, rather than as a specially trained task force, working to professional standards simply in order to make its service more effective. The humblest and—in the ecclesiastical sense— Lowest Congregational or Methodist chapel is as vulnerable

[1] *The Recovery of Unity* (Longmans, 1958), p. 6.
[2] *The Protestant Ministry* (Faber, 1958), p. 37.

as any to priestcraft, even if it possesses no ordained minister to play the role of the priest, for it can and usually does allow the very absence of a minister to limit unnecessarily the ministry of its members, both in the church and in the community. Such chapels, indeed, quite often openly put forward their lack of a paid, professional minister as an excuse for their introversion. 'We can't possibly do this . . . study this . . . attend that. We haven't got a minister.' The corrosive influence is especially visible in these churches' pattern of worship. Whoever is actually conducting the services, ordained minister or visiting lay preacher, the pattern is irretrievably sacerdotal, the congregation neither speaking by itself nor performing an action from start to finish. Even the Lord's Prayer is commonly 'led' in a loud voice from the pulpit, presumably in case the congregation forgets the words.

The Church Order of Dissent

Once, English Dissent was not in danger of succumbing to these errors, and the history of how they arose in the Free Churches has some relevance to our understanding of what has to be got rid of. English Puritanism, from its sixteenth-century origins to its seventeenth-century flowering, was in intention at least a theocracy, devised on the assumption of equal status—indeed, equal priesthood—among all believers. Ultimately, the hope of many was to theocratize English society, if not on the pattern of Calvin's Geneva then on some other pattern, and the debates in Cromwell's army at Putney in 1647, with their intermittent adjournments for prayer, remind us that in this period even tough, democratically inclined men, arguing fiercely in public about the social order they wanted for their country, accepted (at least outwardly) the duty to refer their findings to the judgement of the Holy Spirit. This had consequences at which we glanced in the last chapter. Dissenting church government assumed a literate, inquiring, theologically educated community which, for all its reliance on ministerial preaching as an indispensable guide to the truth, was unwilling to surrender its private and communal right to search the Scriptures on its own behalf, with its own moral and intellectual resources. Puritan laymen, apart from the Quakers on their left wing, wanted ministers and had a clear function in mind for them, but were in no danger, either as churchmen or as citizens, of abdicating their own responsibility as they saw it.

But by the time of the Evangelical Revival, the form of ecclesiastical settlement in England had long since been decided. Wesley's message was about individual holiness, not communal order, and its effect on the social order of England itself was an accidental by-product, not a foreseen consequence, of what was said in Methodist pulpits. Laymen were—and are—extensively used by Methodism, but it is significant that their characteristic use has been as 'lay preachers' who were—and are—regarded more as substitutes for the ordained clergy than as ministers possessing special gifts and opportunities precisely because they are laymen. In the old days, these men took the talent for public speaking which they acquired and fostered in the pulpit into the political life of their locality, but they did not, as the Puritans would have done, try to carry over from the ecclesiastical to the secular sphere any particular theory of how a church or a society should be ordered. Rather, they carried into the Church from the secular sphere many of the assumptions of popular democracy, because their evangelical pietism possessed no intellectual apparatus to criticize these assumptions. It is not self-evident that 'one man, one vote' is the foundation principle of theocratic church order, and the Quakers, at least, still use the more excellent way, counting heads only as a last resort. But during the nineteenth-century and its aftermath democratic shibboleths became fixed, not only among Methodists, but also among the Orthodox Dissenting bodies influenced by the Evangelical Revival, Congregationalists and Baptists. Hence what happened to the Congregational 'church meeting', the characteristic feature of Independent church government, designed to express the absolute authority of Christ over the people of his covenant. More and more, during the nineteenth century, this assembly for waiting on the will of God became an instrument whereby a congregation could impose its own 'democratic' will on its minister or on a dissident, no doubt sometimes prophetic, minority in its midst. This corruption was followed by almost total atrophy, until most members of most Congregational churches came to regard their church meetings simply as necessary but burdensome democratic institutions, like the town council or the golf club committee, which they attended if they were interested in the conduct of church business, but not if they were not. Despite a recent quickening of interest, this is still generally the case today.

I have mentioned one of the influences which has been driving the Free Churches towards introversion, discouraging their laymen, however zealous and conscientious in 'serving' their church and keeping it intact as an institution, from any communal attempt to penetrate in the name of the Gospel the secular society in which they spend most of their time and which usually possesses their allegiance at the deepest level. But there is at least one other associated historical influence which propels us in the same direction. This is the traditional Dissenting conception of the local church as the company of people in that place who have been 'gathered' out of the world by Christ to follow him. On this theory, the local church and the local community cannot be regarded as in any sense coterminous, unless *all* citizens have made this conscious commitment of themselves to the worship and service of the church, and this, though logically possible, is practically remote. This basic belief, in varying forms, is common to all Dissenting denominations in Britain, and is naturally reflected in the forms of church order which they have adopted. Many outside the ranks of Dissent agree that it expresses one important truth about the Church. But it was an insight which took root among English Christians at a particular stage of the country's social history, and social history has not stood still since the Tudors. The 'gathered church' system, like all ecclesiastical systems, needs to be measured against society's rapid and radical changes over the last century or so.

I am not here concerned to argue the merits of the 'parish' system, as found in the Church of England, against the 'gathered' system as we have it in the Free Churches. The parish system still has its strengths in many situations, if properly used, and men such as Ernest Southcott in Halton, Leeds, have shown that it can even be used as a launching pad for fresh probes into the fragmented life of modern cities.[1] But over Britain as a whole it has broken down, and as long as Christianity in this country remains the preoccupation of a small minority, disunited among itself, parish churches will remain what they usually are today, gathered churches under a different name. Instead of pursuing a sterile debate about the respective merits of Anglican and Dissenting ecclesiastical machinery, we would do better to listen to the sharp questions put by Dr Cunliffe Jones:

> Is the Church willing to reconsider the traditions of 'the parish church' and 'the gathered church' from within the privilege and opportunity of a technological society? It may be that God has a use for either or both of these conceptions within such a society. But it is one thing from within the new gifts of God to mankind through a technological society to reconsider inherited traditions. It is quite another thing to insist that God cannot allow the world to change to such an extent that inherited Church structures ought to be reconsidered. It is certain that God does not run the universe with a special tenderness to the inertia, the timidity or the indecision of His Church.[2]

[1] See his *The Parish Comes Alive* (Mowbrays, 1956).
[2] *Op. cit.*, p. 133.

Still, tradition is strong enough in the Free Churches for it to be necessary to show reason for rejecting the gathered church as the self-evident foundation for the new building that has to be done. The fact is that, just as the 'theocratic' principle of church order presupposed a literate and responsible membership, so the 'gathered' principle presupposed a certain social coherence which is now lacking in most localities. It was assumed, in practice, that the members of a church so constituted would reside in the same neighbourhood. It was no part of the 'gathered' principle that the congregation should be gathered from north and south and east and west for ten miles around. But it was also assumed that members should be neighbours in more than just the residential sense. If their concerns were to be the concerns of the fellowship, if their private anxieties were to be transmuted by the church into outward-looking care, it was necessary for members to live and work, enjoy leisure and offer public service, within sight and sound of each other. Except in some, by no means all, rural communities, this is no longer possible. Unless technological progress is to be rejected wholesale, it is not even desirable. Professor Gibson Winter poses the problem :

In the past century, residential community has been segregated geographically, socially and culturally from the economic and political structures of our society. This segregation of spheres of life in industrial society is the most important fact about social organization in the metropolis ... A man's job is usually related, directly or indirectly, to large organizations of industry and union which have considerable influence on the national life; by contrast, his neighbourhood, life with the family, at church, or in a local association has little or no connection with his job or even with the interests and problems which fill his mind through the day.

Hence, Professor Winter argues, comes the restriction of the Church's functions to solving problems of 'personal inwardness and emotional balance'. In the following passage, there is little difficulty in substituting 'British' for 'American':

> In this sense, 'public worship', as common liturgy in which the richness of the Word and Sacrament intersect with the common life of a people, has disappeared. We simply do not enjoy the experience of public worship, for the intersection of concerns in the religious context does not reflect public matters. To this extent, the proclamation of the Church occurs in an impoverished context which transmutes the Gospel into a superficial reinforcement of the moralistic facade overlaying the American pursuit of private interests . . .
>
> Religious faith and practice have become a private sphere of American life—a sphere preoccupied with the emotional balance of the membership, the nurture of children, and the preservation of a harmonious residential milieu. Protestantism identifies the Church with a 'gathered congregation' of believers, meaning a collection of individuals and families drawn from a specific residential area. Since suburban residential space provides the most stable atmosphere for the support of private interests, Protestantism has flourished in the segregated, suburban islands of private life created by the middle class. Where leisure interests and preoccupation with family values are dominant, religious institutions flourish. Where these values are undermined by inner city life, the ministry of the churches evaporates.[1]

It will be noticed how this analysis confirms the trend of our argument. Sub-Puritan Christians in the Free Churches are tempted to become private men, treating their church as a private interest—'much like speedboating or fishing', is Dr Winter's own comparison.[2] We have also suggested that the Free Churches have largely lost their old talent for adult

[1] Op cit., pp. 132-4.

[2] Bishop F. A. Cockin makes the same point: 'There are thousands to whom religion looks like a comparatively harmless

education, for making the great affairs of Church and State, art and social betterment, real within their own four walls; but we have noticed that even dormitory suburbs contain schools, which are at once natural allies of the churches and natural links with the technological society responsible for the existence of the dormitory suburbs. And we are seeing now that assumptions about church order which go un-criticized in an era of rapid social change may be as un-profitable as a lack of any church order at all. In the light of this, the limited success which the Free Churches have re-cently achieved in middle-class suburbs needs careful watching. If it is accompanied, as it often is, by neglect of the inner city and refusal to try conclusions with the princi-palities and powers of the new society, this very success could become the symbol of the Free Churches' marginal position in the country's life.

Nevertheless, it would be no less absurd to abandon the suburbs to their own devices. They are what most of us have to live in. Their character is readily variable, and the poten-tial influence of churches on these variations should not be underestimated. Moreover, men in particular need to re-member that their wives and children—especially their wives —rarely get a chance to escape from their immediate neigh-bourhood, unless for an hour or two's shopping. In the present fluid social and religious situation there is room for many parallel lines of experiment by churches, and in argu-ing, as I shall do, for the secondment of some ministers to charges not based on geographical neighbourhoods and established church buildings, I would want to maintain that an ordinary local church can carve out for itself, if it cares, a complementary area of mission. To its men, the church has to speak and act on the assumption that it is the whole man

---

hobby for those who happen to have that peculiar taste. Others prefer pigeon-fancying, or gardening, or music, or hiking ... '
God in Action (Penguin, 1961), p. 141.

and not just a part of him that is in his pew on a Sunday, and that it is the duty of the fellowship to seek to understand and universalize the problems which each member meets in his daily life. To women, who put into their worship the more intimate affairs of family and neighbourhood, the church on Sunday may need to interpret aspects of the husband's daily life which he cannot or will not communicate himself. And when, as is not at all inconceivable, families go to church to find each other, the 'gathered' community has really 'come alive'.

Only when this happens, or when the need for it to happen is generally appreciated, will there reappear a 'significant lay ministry in denominational Protestantism'. When individuals and families who are turned in on their own affairs band together in churches which are themselves introverted in relation to society (and also in relation to other churches, at home and abroad), there develops within the life of the Church an attitude to the full-time ministry which is superficially subservient but subtly patronizing. The Bishop of Southwell has remarked that if a press photographer wanted to take a picture of the Church at work, he would look for a scene in which parsons were prominently doing something; and Dr Barry added: 'But is that the kind of picture it ought to be, or ought it not to be something quite different—a classroom, perhaps, or a council house or a factory?'[1] The members of the introverted church behave (with less justification) like the press photographer. They are strongly drawn to the secular idea that a minister is a certain sort of person, enjoying a certain status as a reward for the full-time performance of a clearly defined, traditional function. They are drawn to this idea because it leaves their own function no less tidily and narrowly defined. Within those churches whose ministers derive their livelihood directly from the membership, the conception not seldom takes a very nasty

[1] *Part-time Priests?*, p. 12.

turn. The members pay the minister to perform the function which society has outlined for him: preaching, visiting members and adherents, running churchly organizations however otiose. Occasionally they pay him well, if they are generous people who feel guilty about their own affluence, and they are happy to resign into his hands most of the decisions (other than financial ones) which the church has to take. But if the minister's function as he sees it is different from the expectations of his flock, the worse for him. It is necessary to qualify Emil Brunner's dictum:

> The free Churches are forced to play for popularity; in their criticism of social conditions they dare not go to the last ditch; their mouth is stopped by consideration for the members who support them.[1]

It has not always turned out like that, and anyway, as in other departments of the Christian life, it is the possibility of a difficult relationship going awry that justifies the Free Churches' way of maintaining their ministries; for it makes it possible for both ministers and congregations to scale the heights, to demonstrate that even as employees and employers they live under grace, not law. But the relationship does quite often go awry, and it needs to be observed that in exploring unfamiliar spheres of lay mission, no less than in criticizing social conditions, the Free Churches may by the inherited weight of their own systems find it difficult to 'go to the last ditch'.

It is ironic when this direction is taken by churches which nominally subscribe to 'the priesthood of all believers'—a doctrine which is coming to be taken much more seriously by the Church of England than it is in the Free Churches. Mr Robin Denniston, editing the Anglican symposium *Part-Time Priests*, was able to write of his contributors' agreement that 'the supplementary ministry is only a partial manifesta-

[1] *The Divine Imperative* (Lutterworth Press, 1947), p. 550.

tion of the need to express the priesthood of all believers'.[1]
At present, of course, the Anglican vicar's near-monarchical
rule in his church, and his exaggerated status in society, still
often result in an Anglican congregation's possessing a
power of veto—that is, 'they can always stay away'—but
little power of initiation. However, in Dissenting churches
parsons who behave as absolute monarchs are not quite such
rare birds as we like to think, and there are very many congregations who behave as though they were, or wished they
were, led by a benevolent dictator who would as far as possible 'be the Church' himself and leave the laity alone, so to
speak, with their snapshot albums. Instead of calling a minister 'to equip the saints for their own work of ministry'
(Ephesians 4.12)—to perform, that is, the functions dele-
gated to him in recognition of his special training and skills
—they define their own tasks as what is left over when the
minister (and of course his wife) have done theirs. It is a
debatable matter whether it is the mistakes of our fathers
and grandfathers, the pressures of society, or inherent faults
in Dissenting church order, which have brought us to this
pass. Probably it is all three. But it is the way back that
matters, and unfortunately, one of the aspects of our predicament is that the vast majority of congregations, theologically illiterate and incapable of striking out on their own,
depend utterly on the ordained ministry to point out the
path and set them on it. But by and large, the Free Church
ministry today is in no condition to do this.

Ministers Today

Viewing the Free Churches collectively, it may be roundly
stated that there are too many ministers, of very uneven
quality, patchily trained and appallingly paid to work at the
wrong jobs in the wrong places. I take these points in no
particular order.

The suggestion that there are too many ministers in the

[1] p. 136.

Free Churches will inevitably shock those who spend their days appealing for ordination candidates to come forward so that the growing number of vacant pastorates may be filled. Perhaps it needs re-phrasing. There are, then, too many churches, and more ministers serving them than we have any right to expect. The Baptist leader J. H. Shakespeare said this memorably in 1916, as part of an appeal for Free Church unity, and although the appeal has for both good and bad reasons been refused, the point has lost nothing of its force in forty-five years. The apparent 'shortage' of ministers is largely a result of the wasteful, selfishly sectarian and generally un-Biblical use to which Free Church ministers are commonly put. This use itself stems often from the un-planned, over-optimistic expansionism of nineteenth century Nonconformists, building pretentious, shoddy churches which were even in those days barely able to sustain a full-time ministry. When so much needs to be changed in these churches as they survive today, from their spiritual condition to their geographical situation, it is ungracious to imply, as is often done, that all would be well were it not for the in-comprehensible reluctance of men to enter the ministry. It is possible, indeed, that men are not as reluctant as they are made out to be. No one has calculated, so far as I know, how many ordination candidates a given number of church-goers may fairly be expected to produce in an age when the ministry is no longer the obvious destiny of a talented and idealistic young man. But it is relevant here to point out that in 1961 the Church of England ordained the largest number of men (626) that she has ordained since 1912. Averaged out over the last four years, the ratio of ordinations to Christmas communicants is 1:3,367. In the English Free Churches over the past four years, Methodists have ordained 105, Congregationalists 50, Baptists 43 and Presbyterians 7 (yearly average).[1] As a ratio to current church membership figures,

[1] English Presbyterians traditionally import many ministers from other Presbyterian churches in the British Isles.

these work out as 1 : 6,939, 1 : 4,136, 1 : 7,532 and 1 : 10,155 respectively.[1] Which of these denominations is shortest of ministerial candidates—the one which comes off worst on these figures, or the one which complains the most of the trouble it has filling vacant pastorates? When a denomination finds that 'too few' candidates are offering for its ministry, it should not merely ask for more, but rather ask itself why it thinks there are too few, and scrutinize with redoubled care the ones who do offer. For if the times are evil, if social change is rapid, if morale is low, and if the need for the Church to be adaptable is more pressing than it has ever been, this is no time to be ordaining third-raters, who by the time they are forty will be only fit to ply the oil-can in a defensive way to denominational machinery which should have been on the scrap-heap years ago.

This is not to say that the work which there is to do does not demand, over the Church as a whole, an increased rate of recruitment to the ordained ministry. Nor can the Church of England, aiming through its parish system at blanket coverage of the entire country, congratulate itself when it realizes that it possesses today 4,000 fewer priests than it possessed in 1900. The harvest is great and the labourers are few. But the tasks to which today's recruits are being set

[1] There is no statistic which gives a satisfactory basis of comparison between the Church of England and the Free Churches; and until someone takes the trouble to collect a reliable week-by-week church attendance figure there will not be. But Anglican Christmas communicants (fewer in number than Easter communicants) probably take their churchmanship not much less seriously than the aggregate of names on Free Church membership rolls, which are often hopelessly unrealistic. Assuming this to be so, in the Church of England there is one minister to every 135 churchgoers; in the Methodist Church one to every 235; in the Presbyterian Church of England one to 246; in Congregational churches one to 157; and in Baptist churches one to 151.

resembles less the reaping of a harvest than the cultivation of a back garden, and their general docility in this employment only makes it easy for the laity to burke the fact that the employment itself is radically miscalculated. The so-called problem of ministerial manpower in the Free Churches would be greatly diminished if these churches could be seen to be recruiting for inherently apostolic forms of ministry, whether within or without the privatized circle of established congregations.

The defects in the quality and the training of the ministers we have are an even more delicate matter. Some would hold that young ministers are better equipped intellectually than they were forty years ago, even if they lack the heroic characteristics displayed by the classes of, say, 1880-1900. Again, it can be claimed with much justice that Free Church theological colleges today are healthier, less enclosed institutions than they were, and that the intellectual invasion of Barth and Niebuhr has dissipated in the colleges much of the woolliness from which the churches are still suffering.

Perhaps the truth of the matter is that there have indeed been improvements, both in the attainments of ministerial candidates and in the way these attainments are developed by theological colleges, but that the improvements are in no way commensurate with the changes in society itself.[1] My last chapter drove to the conclusion which I draw here, that only an altogether exceptional man is fit to be ordained into the full-time ministry of the Free Churches today if he has not been educated to graduate level before he starts his ministerial training. And the logic of the meritocratic society which we are entering is that there will be fewer and fewer

[1] D. R. Davies, who described racily in *In Search of Myself* (Bles, 1961) his own chequered experience of the Congregational ministry between the wars, argued strongly that Dissenting ministers, often compelled by poverty to spend time augmenting their salaries, are even now not meeting the 'heavy intellectual demands' of 'a disintegrating society' (pp. 200-202).

'exceptional men' who will fail to be selected for university education. There is, practically speaking, no such animal in modern society as the 'natural' minister. There are, most definitely, people who are natural selections for the intensive spiritual and intellectual training which a pastoral minister needs today if his light is not to go out with disastrous results long before he retires, *circa* 2000 A.D. Nor is it possible to make silk purses out of sows' ears, Christian ministers out of people who are at heart bored by their fellowmen. But that is a different matter.

These pressures are naturally felt by those who decide the content of the training which Free Church ordinands are to receive. One has every sympathy with both parties. All educationists today are hag-ridden by the absolute necessity of teaching their pupils, in whatever discipline, too much in too little time. Students are to specialize, they are not to specialize too much; they are to be literate, numerate, vocationally competent, civically conscious, emotionally developed and generally educated to near-Baconian standards, all within the span of years allotted to their particular intelligence level and field of study. It is of the essence of the Christian ministry that these same pressures are doubled and redoubled within its own scheme of training, for how else can the minister be 'all things to all men'?

It is, of course, an impossible task, with the result that it is seldom even attempted. It would take a combination of Aquinas and Leonardo to approach the intellectual and spiritual variousness which is theoretically demanded of the contemporary ministry. Allowing the conventional three years for the basic study of Greek, church history, doctrine, liturgy, preaching, pastoral psychology and denominational church order, it might be considered absurd to allow a man into the pastoral ministry without the mental and emotional equipment of the social caseworker (two years), the craft of the teacher (one year), a firm grasp of politics, economics and at least one natural science (say four years), and a year or two in some secular employment to blow away the academic cobwebs. Ridiculous as this programme sounds—and even so it leaves out the need throughout to allow time for prayer and reflection—there is no avoiding the need either for a scaled-down version of it, or for a degree of specialization which has not so far commended itself to denominations which look askance at ministers not in charge of churches, and concede only reluctantly that there may be room in the system for the consultant as well as the general practitioner. Mr D. L. Munby recently touched on this point in discussing the failure of the Church to give relevant and technically competent guidance on economic and ethical issues:

'Perhaps the fundamental failure is the failure to see that the problem is one of organization. Too often the Church strikes the layman as a set of one-man competing shows, each run by one man, good, bad, or indifferent. . . . One of the virtues of an episcopal system is that it enables experiments to be carried out under the aegis of the bishop, by special people appointed for the task, whereas a presby-terian' [and *a fortiori*, a congregational] 'system, whose ministry is essentially parochial, is not well equipped for dealing with the kind of problem I have in mind. But not all bishops realize the advantages they are blessed with. . . .'[1]

Traditional Dissenting forms of church order, in fact, need thorough questioning in a society which has had to centralize many of its institutions, and institutionalize many of its formerly haphazard initiatives, in order to prevent total economic and social fragmentation. Perhaps it is the failure to diagnose these difficulties, and make a conscious choice between the alternative procedures available, which is parti-ally responsible for the crop of 'accidents' which seem to be-fall young Dissenting ministers in the years after leaving college. Statistics are not to be found in this connection, but

[1] *God and the Rich Society* (Oxford, 1961), p. 169.

one's personal impression is that a great many such men enter their first churches pathetically unprepared for the everyday terrors and complexities of the task, especially in the field of human relations, and either muddle through their lives with congregations which are themselves too immature to discern what is wrong, or make a swift escape into teaching and other secular or semi-secular employments. Even here, one wonders how they make out, especially in teaching; for to judge by their behaviour when they are asked to lead a study group, chair a meeting, or just listen, Dissenting ministers are often all too ready to accept that they are running one-man shows.

An Aim for the Free Churches

But clearly, reforms of ministerial training, and steadfast refusal to 'dilute' the entry, are in themselves useless without ruthless appraisal of the institutional function which ministers are expected to discharge in the Church and in society as a whole. This raises the question, fundamental not just to this chapter but to the whole inquiry: what sort of institutions should the Free Churches seek to be, if it is granted that at present they are not just bad examples of the right kind of institution, but in some respects good examples of the wrong kind? What sort of activities and ministries, clerical and lay, ought they to be fostering during the interim period before organic reunion with each other and the Church of England (the precondition of real advance) begins to become a practical possibility? If Dr Cunliffe-Jones, himself not normally regarded as a revolutionary in matters of church order, feels that both parish and gathered systems are today inadequate, how are they to be supplemented or replaced? And if it is admitted that most lay members of Free Churches conceive their own function far too narrowly, how are they to learn to behave once more like the responsible theocracy, the believers' priesthood, which in their lucid intervals they claim to be?

In the short space available here, there is no hope of returning a systematic answer to these questions, but some points
may be made. There is, for instance, the problem of Free
Church distribution. Almost all communities in Britain
which are of a size to support a chapel have one, and many
such communities have half a dozen. Although the Roman
Catholics in this country have shown us that it may be much
easier for a Christian communion to expand with fewer focal
points for its loyalty, it is probably right, given the modes of
growth and assembly, 'the family feeling', which come
naturally to Dissenters, that this expansion into new suburbs
and towns should continue. There may not be much whole-
ness about these new communities, and their male residents'
centre of gravity may be found elsewhere. But to neglect
them would not only be to leave the old, the young, and the
housebound virtually unchurched; it would be to forgo a
natural laboratory of mission, a place where people can
and must be reached and served and educated in new ways
because they have made a clean cut from old habits and
environments. But there are at least two conditions to be
met first.

One is that the work of church extension, though usually
limited by agreement with the local authority to one particular denomination in any one area, should not actually be
undertaken only by one denomination but by as many as can,
in local circumstances, be marshalled to help. The logic of
the decision not to poach each other's territories, which the
Free Churches have already arrived at in relation to new
estates, demands no less. This does not mean that the re-
sultant church should be 'undenominational'—as if such a
thing were possible—but that its interdenominational helpers
and members should essay to make it a good church of the
tradition which has been appointed, a visible demonstration
that it is confessional loyalty which marries best with the
ecumenical spirit.

The second condition is an open acknowledgment from

top to bottom of the Free Churches that suburban advance and downtown recovery, even when they are achieved, are not enough; that for some of its members, the local church is the base camp, not the front line; and that the forward positions are being overrun for lack of skilled manpower. From those who defend what they erroneously imagine to be classic Independency, the cry will perhaps be heard that any demotion of the local church, bricks, mortar and all, means more centralized control. In the sense that it is hard to see how more Biblical forms of mission can be financed without such control, this is fair. But in another sense, the result of the reform would be the break-up of ecclesiastical institutions into smaller units, not greater. The Christian cell in a factory or a professional circle, funding its own activities, deciding its own pattern of work, studying the Bible and perhaps celebrating the Lord's Supper as an entity on its own, comes very much closer to Independency as Robert Browne saw it than the unholy isolationism of a prosperous suburban church, with 200 members who scarcely know each other by sight. If a sizeable proportion of the Free Church ministry were enabled to become itinerant once again—not necessarily itinerant in the geographical sense, but itinerant in the complex mazes of contemporary society, fathers in God to Christian organisms evolved by the lay men and women who spend their lives in these mazes— new heart would be put into both ministry and laity, and incidentally, new impetus given to the search for Christian unity.[1] As it is, however, it has been left largely to the Church of England to explore new functions for its ministers, and new ministries for its laymen.

This may be partly because the history and organization of the chapels does not require them, as it at least theoretic-

---

[1] One is aware that the Methodist ministry, whose ministers are moved on every five years or so from one group of static churches to another similar group, is quaintly called 'itinerant'.

ally requires parish churches, to seek out people where their treasure and their hearts are to be found. But probably the chief reason why Free Church ministers have undertaken so few such experiments in evangelism is that local churches have refused to pay for them. This is quite understandable. The General Assembly of the Church of Scotland in 1961 argued long and earnestly whether or not to appoint its *first* full-time industrial chaplain, and even Anglican bishops have to go cap in hand to their dioceses before they can raise money for new ventures among young people or factory workers. Yet Anglican parishes, thanks to the Church Commissioners' adroit service of God and Mammon simultaneously, have an immense money potential beside Dissent, which has to pay its ministers out of its freewill offerings, and sustain its church extension and total home and foreign mission out of what is left. For some Dissenters this means a type of sacrifice still largely unknown in parish churches. For most, however, not; and the sacrifice is not general enough for Free Church ministers to need to be paid, as they are, on the cheap. It may be right to insist that the Protestant minister ought not to act as though his church owed him a living, but this does not mean that his church ought to answer his modesty with a slap in the face. But this is what most current Nonconformist ministerial stipends amount to.

In many of the pioneering ministries for which room needs to be made in the Free Churches, the pastor would, like St Paul, be able to thank God that he was no charge on his flock, for he would earn much of his living in secular employment, becoming, according to skill, vocation and training, either a 'part-time priest' or a fully-fledged 'worker priest'. But however enterprising the Free Churches were suddenly to become in this respect, the ministry in the 'local church' would inevitably remain the typical ministry, and it should be rewarded according to the demands made upon it. Churches expect their ministers to marry, and their wives to do 'church work'; much of it grindingly dull. They expect at least a proportion of sons of the manse to grow up with enough respect for their fathers' employers to hear the same call themselves. They expect, even if they do not always appreciate, professional standards, and like to see their minister moving as an equal among the leaders of his community. At today's prices £1,000 a year plus a free house is probably the minimum that such a man ought to be paid after a probationary period, and it is only sentimentalized and usually inconsistent notions about the ideal of 'holy poverty' which enable congregations to pay their ministers less.

The undisputed fact that very many churches could not immediately afford to pay their ministers such a sum only supports the thesis. Such churches would have several alternatives, all potentially fruitful, from which to choose. They could close their doors and go elsewhere—and for many fellowships, this act would be their last hope of regaining spiritual health. They could, if they had not yet reached that point of no return, share a minister with other churches, as the Methodists do, but unlike Methodists, allow their life to be shaped round the secular placement of their members rather than round the maintenance of the church building and its weekly services. They could become, if they were poor but strategically important, a charge on richer churches. Even in the most atomized Dissenting denominations, this process has been a feature of the post-war period, but it has not gone nearly far enough, and it is of some symbolic importance that the ministers in charge of these points of growth are generally the worst paid.

Their last alternative, of course, would be to raise their incomes to the required level. It is probable that the spectacular successes of Anglican stewardship campaigns cannot be equalled by Free Churches: the Anglicans, after all, started from an extremely low level of giving, and with a vast latent constituency of non-churchgoing wellwishers. The widening gap between rich and poor in our society extends to denominations as well as to individuals. But it is worth observing that the Mormons, who are at present proselytizing most effectively among dissatisfied and uninstructed Dissenters, tithe their income before tax to their sect. Put it less strenuously, and assume that fifty earning members of a congregation, each with a disposable income of £1,000 per annum, gave a twentieth of that sum to the Church. Even this comes to £2,500—more if the gifts were covenanted. Heaven forbid that money on this scale should be made instantly available to certain large and prosperous Free Churches in their present spiritual malaise, for they would most probably bring the Christian faith into public contempt by the massive selfishness with which they spent it. It is indicative of Christian priorities as they are understood in this country that whereas in 1908, 11.9 per cent of Anglican parish expenditure in England went to the Church's overseas mission, in 1958 the proportion was 4.6 per cent; and only the lack of figures for the Free Churches hides a similar declension.[1] But the danger of inordinate affluence, real enough in American church life, at present only needs to be noted here. The degree of sacrifice and enthusiasm which would be required before giving in the Free Churches could be raised to these levels would itself be some guarantee of proper attention being paid to the objects on which the money was spent. It is clear that every local church would have a duty to tithe, indeed much more than tithe, its income to Christian and humanitarian objects outside its own direct control.

The biggest single obstacle to the revolution which all this would involve is loyalty—the loyalty of the individual Dissenter, not to his faith, not even to his denomination, but

[1] But the statistics, even if available, would not be comparable. Responsibilities for paying the clergy differ. As a percentage of chapel income after payment of the minister's salary, missionary expenditure by chapels is almost certainly over 5 p.c. Equally certainly, the proportions used to be higher.

to the chapel in which he was bred, or which he has helped to sustain over many years. This loyalty has its admirable aspects, and without it in the lean years of the recent past many fellowships could hardly have survived. Nevertheless, one cannot but welcome the loosening of these hoops of steel which the social mobility of the times is bringing, for broadening experience makes it impossible to see any single church, however active or worshipful, as the *summum bonum*. Eventually, perhaps, it may open our ears to Daniel Jenkins' reminder that the effectiveness of church members is not to be judged by the amount of time they spend in the service of the sanctuary, or in attendance on their minister:

> The minister is the servant of his people, who has to help them discern for themselves the will of God for their real work in the real world. It will often be his duty, therefore, to establish a certain economy in the internal life of the Church, so that people are released to give time and energy to fulfilment of their Christian duty in the worlds of industry or politics or business or professional life, where their most determinative decisions have to be taken. A new puritanism is urgently needed in most churches, which cuts away ruthlessly from their life all organizations and activities which prevent their members from grappling with their real task.[1]

The great merit of the Free Churches as institutions is that once they have learnt a lesson, they are able to apply it quickly and without more ado to their actual practice. In this sense they can afford to give the Anglican reformers a head start. But there are as yet few signs that the learning process has begun.

[1] *The Protestant Ministry*, p. 112.

V

DISSENT OR ASSENT?

All protestantism, even the most cold and passive, is a sort of
dissent. But the religion most prevalent in our northern colonies
is a refinement on the principle of resistance: it is the dissidence
of dissent, and the protestantism of the Protestant religion
Edmund Burke.

THE central point at issue in the last chapter was this: what
ways can be found for Dissenting churches and their ministers to mesh with the secular institutions of modern society?
But the answer, in so far as an answer was possible, could
only be an interim one, for it waited on the answer to a more
searching question: Are there to be Dissenting churches at
all, or is there to be, in the lifetime of some of us, a united
Church in England which will embrace at least all the non-
Roman traditions represented here? Is it, in short, to be Dissent or Assent? Is it still a case of—as the old temperance
ditty puts is——'have courage, my boy, to say no'? Or does
anything much matter now except the positive affirmations
which after 300 chequered years we are able and obliged to
make about the religious experience which has been vouch-
safed to us, and about the good ordering of Christian communities? It is a much-quoted saying of Archbishop Temple's
that denominations are usually 'right in what they affirm
and wrong in what they deny'. The reason is simple: the
affirmation is based on experience, the denial all too often
on unalloyed ignorance (vide the correspondence columns of
all religious journals, of whatever ecclesiastical colour). The
Reformers and the Puritans, it should be remembered, con-

centrated their 'denial' and rejection on beliefs and practices which they knew from the inside to be false and corrupting. We, their successors, so often merely construct a mental image of the traditions from which we are separated, and ourselves reject the image rather than the contemporary reality.

However, on the whole it is now only a few atavists in the Free Churches who are quite unable to concede that 'we know in part and prophesy in part'. The atavists are not just an inconvenience but a genuine theological problem, to which I return. But they are not the main problem, which in the English situation is now being identified as primarily institutional. We have got to the stage in this country where, if it were left to the theologians, the reunion of the Church would be considerably farther forward than it is. It is not the ayes and the noes which are weighing most heavily in the ecumenical scale at present: it is the don't-want-to-knows, who are—in the Free Churches at any rate—generally also don't-want-to-knows in regard to their own denomination's doctrine and church order. This is why it has been necessary to question how far the truths about man and God, Church and society which Dissent has discovered by experience, and holds in trust for the coming Great Church, are in fact still on display in the Free Churches as contemporary human institutions. And further, we have to recognize that there are two ways in which these truths could disappear from our ken. On the one hand, they might disappear in a mis-handled, total absorption of the Free Churches, separately or collectively, by some other communion (in the English context, necessarily the Anglican communion). It is a measure of the Free Churches' present lack of confidence in their own spiritual strength and identity that this should be their main fear at present. On the other hand, the same truths could disappear simply through the ossification of the institutions to which they were originally entrusted. It would be a rash man who discounted this possibility altogether when he reflects on what the social upheavals of the last fifty years have done to Dissent, and then projects his imagination into the even greater upheavals which are likely in the half-century which lies ahead. Nor is it safe to point to the undoubted achievements of isolated churches and individual ministers in regaining touch with their environment and at the same time recapturing their own confessional tradition in all its freshness. For in the end, under modern conditions, their work loses most of its effect unless the revival extends to the denomination as a whole, the institution which claims their allegiance and often enough finds much of the money for their activities.

The Ecumenical Pressure

In the last fifty years there has at least been one solid gain, one unmistakable afflatus of the Holy Spirit, for Christians to set against their losses, and that is the ecumenical movement. I do not intend to swell the gush of self-panegyric which this development too readily evokes from churches which have not sensed its full implications; better, surely, to treat it as a natural, glorious, but overdue and grossly incomplete rediscovery of the Gospel, and to insist that the reunion of the Church, like world government, is an object whose attainment will require not dedication and prayer alone, though these are primary, but foresight and fasting. But one general point about the ecumenical movement bears making at the present time. It is normal for ecumenists to profess shock that the movement is now fifty years old without our seeing more than one major scheme of reunion bear fruit.[1] As a rebuke to our hardness of heart, this is entirely justified. But history may surely judge it providential that the impulse to reunite the fragmented Church began where and when it did, that its roots were in days of confidence rather than of despair, and that so much thought

[1] See e.g., Kenneth Slack, *The British Churches Today* (SCM Press, 1961).

and effort and prayer had to be offered by the best Christian minds of two generations, before the Church as a whole became aware that there was an ecumenical movement at all. For if the longing for unity were simply the creation of the past decade, the public at large could hardly help regarding it simply as a proposed merger between several old-established firms whose profits were declining. Fortunately, there is no excuse for so regarding it. The pressure for reunion came from the mission field at a time when the British churches had great confidence in their mission, and were enjoying the fruits of a religious boom (the last fruits, but they were not to know this in 1910). Consequently, reunion has throughout been studied, not as administrative convenience or sentimentally-approved togetherness, but as obedience to the Dominical injunction that our oneness should mirror the oneness of the Father and the Son. What this means, translated into terms of our church life, was comprehensively stated by the World Council of Churches in 1961 :

> We believe that the unity which is both God's will and his gift to his Church is being made visible as all in each place who are baptized into Jesus Christ and confess him as Lord and Saviour are brought by the Holy Spirit into one fully committed fellowship, holding the one apostolic faith, preaching the one Gospel, breaking the one bread, joining in common prayer, and having a corporate life reaching out in witness and service to all; and who at the same time are united with the whole Christian fellowship in all places and all ages in such wise that ministry and members are accepted by all, and that all can act and speak together as occasion requires for the tasks to which God calls his people.
> It is for such unity that we believe we must pray and work.

Thus, despite the bottomless ignorance which very many Anglicans and Free Churchmen show both of the demand which is made and of the response which has so far been made to it, neverthless it is possible to take much for granted about the foundations which have been laid. In framing plans and discussing probabilities, in urging the Free Churches, individually and collectively, to shape a conscious strategy, perhaps even complete with timetables, towards the various alternative or complementary forms of reunion possible in this country over the next half-century, we ought to be able to avoid laying ourselves open to the charge that we are indulging in sordid and unspiritual calculation. Indeed, where the Free Churches' attitude to unity has in the past gone wrong, it has often been possible to diagnose the fault as a falsely-spiritualized concept of what is involved. It is falsely spiritual, for example, to suppose that anything of more than *conditional* significance has occurred if separated Christians sit or kneel together at the Lord's Table while remaining, and intending to remain, apart in their church order, their social life, and their outreach to the non-Christian world. Rather, they eat and drink judgement to themselves.[1]

There are further reasons for seeking organic reunion which also derive from the Bible, but less directly. The Bible could scarcely be more insistent that Christianity is not a never-never religion, timeless, passionless, and gently benevolent. It is almost crudely materialistic, subject to times and

---

[1]The Open Letter to the Archbishops published by 32 Anglican theologians in 1961, asking for more liberal regulations on inter-communion with Dissenters, was in the context of the present regulations not only generous but eminently justifiable. However, it could be – and was – sharply pointed out to the 32 that the inter-communion which the Free Churches had enjoyed among each other for many years had not brought them a whit nearer reunion, and it was small comfort to the Free Churches when one of the Open Letter's instigators, Professor Lampe, replied – and it was hard to contradict him – that this was because the Free Churches had for the most part neglected the centrality of this sacrament in the Church's life.

seasons, to the ebb and flow of historical change. In such a
religion, practical considerations—'mere expediency' is the
pejorative term for the same thing—take on theological significance. 'There are certaine times and seasons wherein God
troubleth the Churches.' Today is not the same thing, theologically speaking, as yesterday or thirty years on. It may be
the appointed time:

> It is common to hear churchmen speak as though they
> did not really regard Christian unity as a serious question
> this side of the End. This is a disastrous illusion. Christians
> cannot behave as though time were unreal. God gives us
> time, but not an infinite amount of time. It is His purpose
> that the Gospel should be preached to all nations, and
> that all men should be brought into one family in Jesus
> Christ. His purpose looks to a real End, and therefore
> requires of us real decisions. If we misconstrue His patience,
> and think that there is an infinity of time for debate while
> we perpetuate before the world the scandal of our dis-
> memberment of the Body of Christ, we deceive ourselves.
> In an issue concerning the doing of the will of God there
> is no final neutrality.[1]

Yet there was strong opposition to the Church of South
India in many quarters, and if the coldest winds blew from
the uplands around Mirfield, there were some chilly breezes
from the fens of Independency. Nearer home, the union of
Congregationalists and English Presbyterians might now be
an accomplished fact but for the tide-turning opposition of
a few denominational leaders when the subject was last dis-
cussed—and at least one of these leaders, to his great credit,
has since admitted that he was mistaken. Similarly, it is arguable that there exists in Britain today a climate of opinion
which is conditionally pro-Christian, wanting to believe but
judging the churches—and it is a very fair criterion—at least
partially on their willingness to resolve their disunity.

[1] Lesslie Newbigin, *The Reunion of the Church* (revised ed.,
SCM Press, 1960), p. xiv.

(Curious that where the Church itself cannot see that unity and mission are different aspects of the same scriptural obliga- tion, the unevangelized masses themselves are pointing it out.) But it is improbable that even this limited receptiveness to sincere and realistic mission will still be found thirty years or fifty years on if no progress towards reunion is made in the intervening period. And even if the people were still receptive, the Free Churches, by then even more remote in time from the social influence and 'common touch' whose lingering effects they still enjoy, would not be able to take advantage of the opportunities presented.

Is there perhaps a warning here to those of us who are concerned with using the mass media to communicate news of, and thought about, the Church? At our peril do we allow our hopes and our desire to please to outrun our sense of reality, our knowledge of the churches as they actually are, for it would be easy to provoke an overpowering public disillusionment with our pretensions. The more widely know- ledge of our concern for unity is disseminated, the less can there be any going back. One wonders whether this aspect of a highly-developed society, in which no institution can keep its business private, is generally appreciated by churchmen.

The Price of Unity

Assuming, then, that visible organic unity in some form is God's will for his Church, and that the partial truths we now hold must find their place in the whole organism before even we ourselves can see their full significance, what adaptations have we to make to the prospect before us? I quote here an Anglican layman, Mr John Lawrence:

There are many tens of thousands of Christians who care for unity, but there are millions who do not. Those tens of thousands have been able to persuade most of 'the historic churches' to pay at least lip service, but how many churches are ready to alter their mode of operation for the sake of unity? Would the Church of England undertake to obtain drastic changes in its relation with the state, if that is a part of the price of unity, and to accept disestablishment if the state refused to make the changes? Would the Roman Catholic Church agree to a vernacular liturgy which drew on Cranmer's translation from the Latin, would it agree to a married clergy, if those things were a part of the price? Would the Free Churches agree to ... well, I would rather the members of the Free Churches put their own questions to themselves.[1]

Taking up the challenge, I suggest the following questions (without supposing for a moment that they are the only ones):

Can we accept emotionally that a united Church means a Church led by bishops and episcopally ordained ministers, and use that acceptance to range ourselves alongside those within the Church of England who want their bishops and ministers to be more scripturally regarded and used?

Can we (this applies especially to Congregationalists and Baptists) emulate the good sense displayed by the United Free Church of Scotland half a century ago, and accept establishment of the Church as a matter for negotiation rather than commination, assured that State recognition of the Christian religion need not detract from the Crown rights of the Redeemer?

Can we so order our worship, preserving spontaneity but banishing accretions of slovenliness and unscriptural habit, that no reasonable Christian man or woman need be scandalized by any of our services?

What follows is little more than an annotation of these points, for I am neither a professional sociologist to discover what Dissenters in their natural habitat do in fact think about the questions I have raised, nor a professional theologian to announce what they ought to think.

[1] *The Hard Facts of Unity* (SCM Press, 1961), p. 112.

1. *Bishops.* As is well known, episcopacy, the ministry and the source of authority in the Church present the most intractable problems, theological and social, in discussions of reunion. When the Church of Scotland was invited by the Report on Conversations between Anglican and Presbyterian Churches to 'make but trial' of bishops-in-presbytery, the heather-root hostility of the Kirk to the very idea—hostility cheered on by strident squawks from the Beaverbrook Press —provided salutary proof that high-level ecumenical encounter between theologically educated people who know and like each other is a very different affair from the clash of closed minds in a fog of suspicion and ancestral fear. The only difference in this regard between the Scottish and the English non-episcopal churches, if the wild sociological generalization may be permitted, is that the English are rather more tolerant, but rather less able to sustain intelligent debate on religious topics.

As to the theological problem, my purpose here is not to describe 'solutions' but to indicate to the reader how the area of disagreement can be broken up, and the sharpest divisions blurred, when people who have a mind to get on with each other are working under a dynamic conception of the Church. I accordingly cite three passages written by men of widely different background and experience: an Anglican suffragan bishop, the principal of a Congregational theological college, and a Church of Scotland missionary who became one of the Church of South India's first bishops and is now an Associate General Secretary of the World Council of Churches.

I am convinced . . . that episcopacy belongs to the *fullness* of the Church, in the sense that the Church will never be fully one, catholic and apostolic until its *episcope* is unified in the historic episcopate. But this is not to say that the *episcope* of Christ has not been, and is not being, exercised in his Body also through other forms of Church order, which may at times give purer expression to it than its current embodiment in the historic episcopate. If we go to the Bible, it must be together to purify our *episcope* (and no *episcope* of the Church which is divided can be truly catholic), not to prove that bishops are, or are not, in the New Testament. In the sixteenth century a return to the Bible divided us: in the twentieth it is uniting us. But it is doing so by forcing us both to a higher and a humbler understanding of the office of a bishop in the Church of God. . . .

Episcope, like priesthood and ministry, is a function of the whole Church. . . . Some of it is best exercised through an individual father-in-God, much of it through the much abused machinery of diocesan administration, that is, through committees and boards of which *laymen* are more often than not the proper chairmen. The ecumenical movement has shown us that episcopal Churches do not necessarily have a monopoly of *episcope* or of episcopal wisdom.[1]

Principal Huxtable comments:

Dr Robinson's suggestion that the various churches should think together about an *episcope* which in some form or other they all share seems providentially opportune; and his statement that the church will never be fully one Catholic and apostolic until its *episcope* is unified in the historic episcopate almost certainly true. The value of his stress is that the discussion can now centre around a common possession which in various ways and in varying degrees we all possess even if in a fragmentary way, whereas hitherto the 'non-episcopal' churches have usually been confronted with the offer of something they almost, if not certainly, lacked.[2]

The third passage is of a rather different nature. It describes what happened to the Church of South India after union had taken place.

When we began to sit down together in councils and

[1] J. A . T. Robinson in *Bishops* (Faith Press, 1961), p. 128.
[2] John Huxtable, *ibid.,* p. 140.

synods to think about our tasks, we found ourselves compelled to examine critically the various patterns that we had inherited. As long as each of us was continuing to run in the grooves that had been provided for us, we were not forced to ask these questions. Precedent settled most matters. But when there were three or four different kinds of precedent to be considered, then deeper questioning became inevitable. We found ourselves looking afresh at the forms of congregational life, of ministry, of lay service which we had inherited; and asking of them 'Is this what God wants us to do in South India today? It may have been right in Europe or America in the eighteenth or nineteenth centuries; is it right for India in the twentieth?' The asking of such questions took us back to the New Testament, and compelled us to begin changing many things that we had taken for granted. We have been forced to think more seriously than we had done before about the congregation as the fundamental unit of Church life, about the diaconate, about the ministry of the laity and especially of women, and about the need for an ordained non-professional ministry of the kind that seems to have been common in the early Church and is still common in some parts of Christendom today. . . .

Undoubtedly many in the non-episcopal churches accepted episcopacy simply because it was one of the things without which union could not be had. Today I think it would hardly be possible to get a vote anywhere for a proposal to drop episcopacy, even as the price of a wider union. The position of the Bishop as the chief pastor of the flock in each area has become something that hardly anyone would wish even to think of abandoning. But on the other hand the Church has a far more open door to the non-episcopal communions than the written text of the Basis of Union suggests . . . I can only interpret these two facts to mean that episcopacy is seen and valued as the visible centre of the process by which the Good Shepherd gathers together His own; and that the desire to see this unifying and reconciling work extended and strengthened overmasters any desire to make claims for episcopacy which would exclude those who are willing to come into the one fellowship.[1]

I do no know whether professional theologians would regard all or any of these passages as significant. They are significant to me, and I think to us all, even more for certain qualities of tone, approach, and vision than for what they actually say. Nevertheless, what they say would fall strangely enough on the ears of the vast majority of devout Christian people in churches and chapels up and down this country, where bishops are regarded (and sometimes regard themselves) as great personages even outside the ecclesiastical sphere, and where vocal minorities on either side of the fence are muttering 'No bishops at any price' and 'Take the historic episcopate—or leave it'. It is hard in such conditions for Dissenters to catch a vision of the 'new model episcopate' as it might serve a united Church, and harder still for them to pay genuine attention when Anglicans speak, however simply and eirenically, of what their episcopal church order has meant to them. I doubt myself if the Free Churches will become convinced that episcopacy is God's will for the Church until a significant and determined company of Free Churchmen, while steadfastly holding that their own non-episcopal communions are fully and really Churches, openly accept episcopacy as the goal and set out, with the help of missionaries and others returning from the Christian frontiers, to expound it at the grass roots. There are some signs that this is happening.[2]

2. *Establishment.* 'It is sometimes hard for a Free Churchman to be sure whether what he dissents from in England is

[1] Lesslie Newbigin, *The Reunion of the Church*, pp. xxix, xxxi. The same author's *South India Diary* (SCM Press, 1951), provides in cheap and small compass a personal, informal and most evocative picture of how these new directions work out in practice for the bishop who watches over them.

[2] Cf. the letter from 29 Methodist ministers and laymen published in *The Guardian* (20.1.62).

Establishment or Episcopacy'. Thus Bernard Manning in his evidence submitted to the Archbishops' Commission on Church and State in 1931.[1] If only to see how this part of the debate between Anglicans and Dissenters has lightened in colour over the past thirty years, Manning's essay bears re-reading, especially at a time when the Church of England is once more rumbling with discontent about the form of her establishment. Indeed, the rumblings have revived an issue which has lately seemed dormant. Our spokesmen have lately been so much concerned with questions of apostolicity and church order that it began to look as though it was really only bishops which divided us. Most of us have already partly forgotten the grievances which were generated in the past by the Church of England's manipulation of her establishment to the detriment of the Free Churches. Christianity in England, closing its ranks against the infidel, has become quite glad to have the State on her side, however lukewarmly. And we are perhaps better able than our fathers were to recognize how little the high theological concerns of such as Manning are by now mirrored in 'the ground floor church' (to borrow a phrase of Ted Wickham's). In chapels up and down the land there are hundreds of thousands of people who effectively dissent from nothing at all, choosing between churches as they would choose between supermarkets, on the basis of what is offered in the way of comfort or inspiration. There are also hundreds of thousands who dissent, not from Establishment or Episcopacy but rather from 'Them'—a composite bogy owing something to both but much to neither, which lurks in the cellars of Dissent's collective unconscious.

However, the general indifference of their constituents to the implications of establishment (which were well understood in the pews a hundred years ago) makes it all the more necessary for denominational leaders to make cool and wise decisions on their behalf when the problem is thrust upon

[1]Republished in *Essays in Orthodox Dissent.*

them by Reunion discussion. Manning's case on Establishment may be briefly summarized thus.

Recognizing that Establishment took many different forms in different countries, and that some forms were infinitely less odious than others, he asserted at the outset that the only tolerable relationship between Church and State secured either 'the predominance of the Church over the State in a theocracy', or 'such an independent equality of Church and State as leaves the Church uncontrolled in its work'. Parliament's dictation to the Church of England over the 1928 Prayer Book was outrageous, but so was the action of Anglican clergymen who enjoyed the advantages conferred on the Church by Parliament and only protested when the price was exacted. Secondly, Manning argued that establishment of the Church was dangerous in a sub-Christian society because it tended to generate over a long period an accumulation of public resentment and anti-clericalism, from which the Free Churches had by their very existence largely saved England. Thirdly, although the political injustices suffered by Free Churchmen had largely been removed, many ecclesiastical injustices remained. 'If we are indeed (and it is the essence of our faith that we are) equally with episcopalians parts of the visible Church, the earmarking of buildings, endowments, university positions and the official representation of Christianity is merely unjust and unjustifiable; and there is no more to be said.' Manning concludes, however, with a personal observation which probably commands more agreement among Dissenters now than it did then.

> Many Free Churchmen have no feeling for the Church of England as a national institution, though they cherish it as a part of Christ's Church; but not a few Free Churchmen, like myself (and I suspect we who feel so are country-bred Free Churchmen), have a tender regard for the Church of England as it now stands as a national institution, while we shrink with some horror from the thought of its being turned into a disestablished, self-governing episcopalian

sect. . . . Self-government, even for the Body of Christ, is a difficult business. We Congregationalists who have given our souls to it for three hundred years in this country are not always very good at it. Episcopalian experiments in self-government in this country fill me with apprehension. . . .[1]

This would be echoed by many in the Church of England itself, usually because they do not trust their ecclesiastical superiors not to pull down historic churches, elect Anglo-Catholic bishops by dozens, emasculate or Romanize the Prayer Book, and generally do everything that is horrid. But it is probably not for Dissenters to worry overmuch about these matters, at least until they are involved in the decisions themselves. And to my mind there is something much more horrid about the Church Society, or any other body of Anglican Evangelicals, lobbying a secularized Parliament to enforce a point of view which has not commended itself to their brethren in church order, than there is about any mistakes which Convocation may or may not make in choosing church officers or revising the liturgy. Most of us, in fact, sympathize whole-heartedly with the Church of England's desire to be allowed to make her own mistakes. But personally, I very much hope that disestablishment (or reestablishment on easier terms) will not be pressed to an issue until reunion in some shape or form is more imminent than it is now. The best guarantee of mistakes not being made by a liberated Church would be the participation of those English Christians who have had three centuries to learn the perils of self-government.

Manning's main points have been softened, though not entirely dissolved, by time. Certain ecclesiastical disabilities have been removed. No Free Churchman can now reasonably complain that Dissent is neglected on State occasions. The 1944 and 1959 Education Acts have—unforeseeably—gone

[1] *Op. cit.,* p. 208.

far to reconcile Dissenters and Anglicans on a subject which once formed the focal point for bitterness about Establishment. Nor need Establishment generate anti-clericalism unless it is forced to express something which goes beyond what most citizens actually feel. A form of Establishment which requires the Queen to be crowned by an Archbishop, and religious instruction to be given in schools, certainly commends itself today to the great majority of English people, and any anti-clericalism that exists can be ascribed almost exclusively to precious, priggish or overbearing behaviour by clerics themselves, of whatever denominational allegiance. But an Establishment, even of a united Church, which gave bishops and clergy rights beyond those they now possess—substantial income tax reliefs, for example—would rightly be repugnant to the electorate.

However, although the Free Churches now take a fairly detached interest in the efforts of their Anglican friends to extricate themselves from humiliating positions vis à vis the State, their concern would become much sharper if reunion took the turn which at least seems possible, and is (as I shall argue in a minute) very much to be hoped for: that is, the union of Anglicans and Methodists as the first stage in the final congruence of the major non-Roman denominations in Britain. In such an eventuality, many grave problems would have to be faced. What agonized cries of betrayal would be heard if ex-Methodist bishops were to be found with their feet up in the House of Lords while the Three Denominations did not even have a life-peer to call their own! Stipend disparity would be a more mundane and pressing source of bitterness. And what of the Church of England's buildings? Generous as Congregationalists and Baptists might wish to be in this matter, and content though they have been to let Anglican clergy and congregations enjoy the use of assets to which their exclusive title is dubious, they could hardly accept as other than very temporary an arrangement which allowed one group of separated Christians the felicity of worshipping again in their parish churches, while other groups, even more deeply rooted in the antiquity of English religion, were denied.[1] Petty and worldly as these objections may sound, it would be a pity if failure to anticipate and meet them compelled the postponement of reunion until an 'umbrella' scheme, covering all the Free Churches simultaneously, became practicable, for as things are this possibility seems remote.

Summing up, the establishment of the Church in England need not present an intractable obstacle to Reunion. Dissenting hostility to Establishment, when properly understood, is directed wholly against the Erastian form of it which has obtained in this country, not against the principle. Religion, after all, has rarely been more firmly established than it was in Calvin's Geneva, from which the prickliest of Dissenters are happy to derive at least part of their church polity. And in so far as it is the principle of the locally autonomous, 'gathered' church which is regarded as incompatible with the vaguer outlines of State-recognized Christianity, we do well to remember that this principle, as it has been worked out in Britain, depends heavily on the simultaneous, geographically coterminous existence of a more centralized and comprehensive ecclesiastical system to fill in the gaps. Bishop Michael Hollis of the Church of South India has pointed out that for Luther and Calvin, as well as for the Anglican Re-

---

[1] This is not just an antiquarian regret. All British communions have been exceptionally slow to conform their new church building to the freshly-rediscovered 'shape of the liturgy'. But the Free Churches have of course been slowest – often for reasons of financial stringency. Consequently, there arise every year new churches (see especially Robert Maguire's St Paul, Bow Common), expressing Puritan insights about worship which the fake gothic chancels of between-the-wars chapels blatantly insult. But, of course, Free Church congregations cannot use these new churches. Such is the waste and anachronism involved in our divisions.

formers, church membership and citizenship were two ways of describing the standing of the same person, and that Independents grew up in reaction against a conception of the Church which they still took for granted as coexisting with their own.

> That becomes very plain when one finds Congregationalists or Baptists faced with the problem of being the Church in an area where, apart from Roman Catholics, there are no other forms of Christianity. This accounts for some of the ways in which in India they differ from the pattern in Britain or North America.[1]

Several quite radical changes, most of which many Anglicans would already welcome, would have to be made in a new form of settlement, and much goodwill would be needed by all three parties to negotiations: Anglicans, Free Churchmen and the State (not to speak of a fourth party, the Roman Catholics, who ought surely to be involved in, for instance, any rearrangement of ecclesiastical representation in the House of Lords). But the most important proviso would be to ensure that whatever agreement was reached was 'open-ended', excluding neither the possibility that Church or State might one day wish to abrogate the agreement, nor the possibility that further denominations or sects, or Rome herself, might one day become involved in a form of establishment mature enough to reflect honestly and generously the tensions and ambiguities involved in citizenship of two cities.

3. *Worship.* This arouses strong emotions because it is what it is, a dialogue between man and God. Christians believe that in praising God for his mighty acts, and in the self-offering that accompanies the praise, men are most truly men. It follows that worship is of all human activities the most vulnerable to corruption—to mechanical repetition, self-deceit, exclusiveness. At deeper levels than is sometimes realized, worship is entangled in the mess of our Christian

[1] *Friends of Reunion Bulletin*, January 1962.

divisions. Our obstinate adherence to the forms to which we are accustomed, and our overt or covert resentment of all others, may reflect (and in extreme cases can be seen to reflect) our inability to come to terms with our own psychologies. But for all its power to raise the devil in us, it is wrong to suppose that worship is a subjective matter. The ascribing of worth to the Most High is not like a love affair, and we properly discuss it in terms of truth and falsity, rather than of 'what feels right for me'.

But here, too, worship divides as well as unites. Professor Horton Davies has observed that Puritanism in England was 'of necessity a liturgical movement. On its positive side it wished to restore English worship to the simplicity, purity and spirituality of the primitive Church. On its negative side it wished to reject those symbols in which Romanism expressed its character'.[1] Because of what worship is, the motives of individual Puritans were no doubt mixed in this matter, as all our motives are. But there can be no doubt that they were correct to subject the worship of the Church to— as it were—a test for verifiability. Worship can be true or false to the Gospel. The Puritans' verifiability principle here was Scripture, and nothing other than Scripture. They were mistaken, I think, in refusing to allow place for other verifiability principles, in departing too far from the tradition of the Church, and in frowning on the free play in worship of the great Christian symbols.[2] But their basic instinct was surely right.

At yet another level, worship is a key topic in the ecumenical dialogue because all Christians take part in it. The ordinary churchgoer may never meet a bishop or a moderator, he may never be personally inconvenienced by establishment or disestablishment, and it is with some difficulty that he com-

[1] *The Worship of the English Puritans* (Dacre Press, 1948), p. 8.
[2] See esp. F. W. Dillistone, *Christianity and Symbolism* (Collins, 1955).

prehends the differences in these regards between his own and other communions. But he worships. And his view of Christian worship outside his own tradition is formed, not by what Anglican or Roman or Methodist or Congregational liturgiologists describe to him as 'characteristic of our worship at its best', but by what he actually encounters when he drops in on St Chad's, or Our Lady of Lourdes, or Cemetery Road Baptist Chapel. For myself, I am fortunate enough to be able to worship happily in the liturgies of several Christian traditions, probably because I became familiar with them at a comparatively early age, even though I feel most completely at home in my own. No one would find it a greater disaster than I if—ridiculous supposition—unity were to result in liturgical uniformity. But never are my latent feelings of hostility towards my fellow-Christians in other communions more thoroughly aroused than when they seem to misunderstand the spirit and misuse the substance of the liturgies which they have received from their fathers in the faith; and never is my indignation with my fellow-Congregationalists stronger than when—as frequently happens—I look for the 'simplicity, purity and spirituality' which men died to obtain, and find it overlaid with slovenliness, superstition and sentimentality. If the Free Churches wish their worship to be coveted by Anglicans and Roman Catholics, and by Quakers and Salvationists, for the various liturgies of a united Church, a fresh Puritan revolution is needed in many of the chapels which wax most defensive about what they suppose to be the 'Nonconformist tradition'.

Particularly does this apply to our celebration of the sacrament of the Lord's Supper. Here again I cannot forbear to quote Manning:

> The witness of the Reformation has perished among us when the glory of the primitive rite is lost. Have you never been at a Communion service where the bread and the wine, handed to us from the Upper Room itself, were

treated as tiresome, rather unspiritual adjuncts to a service, impedimenta to be disposed of as rapidly and inconspicuously as possible lest they should hinder us (God forgive us) from spiritual flights on our own account? Have you never received the Sacrament when those august and primitive actions which the Reformers were burnt to win for us from the confused millinery of the Mass are not now thought worth repeating? Have you not known them wantonly and heartlessly neglected, though they carry us back to our Redeemer Himself more surely than any spoken word or any unspoken thought? The bread and the wine are sometimes huddled round to us before the service proper begins, or perhaps under cover of some hymn. The bread is not broken. The wine is not poured out. Prayer, thanksgiving, and the invocation of the Holy Ghost do not precede the distribution of the Elements. . . . In some places and at some times these things are done; and everyone knows that that is true.[1]

The full range of these horrors is now not often found. In colleges and places where they theologize, and sporadically in the churches at large, there has been a recovery of the Reformers' sacramental doctrine. But if 'unity in each place' is to become more than a phrase, Free Churchmen everywhere need to subject their communion services, above all, to the most rigorous and imaginative scrutiny, asking themselves whether there is adequate scriptural warrant for practices which would scandalize Christians who belong to other traditions. I deliberately select a trivial-seeming example which yet cuts deep. Is it too much to ask that we should imitate our Puritan forefathers (not to speak of John Wesley), and accustom ourselves at Communion to drink real wine from a single cup, rather than ersatz grape juice from individual medicine glasses? Is it not a measure of our failure to comprehend this sacrament and its conveyance to us of liberating, abounding grace that we are prepared to abandon

[1] *Essays in Orthodox Dissent*, p. 61.

these intimate links with the Last Supper for a social scruple about alcohol which St Paul saw no reason to enjoin even on the drunken communicants of Corinth? I am aware that in Methodist churches unfermented wine at Communion is at present mandatory, by direction of Conference, and is often used in other denominations' services too. In a most interesting sociological survey of Anglican-Methodist relations in two Sheffield parishes it is recorded that one of the Methodist women interviewed 'thought the Anglican Church should make its members be teetotal before allowing Holy Communion'.[1] The merits or demerits of total abstinence as such are not in point here, but in so far a a particular social judgement is generalized in Dissenting worship as a new circumcision, a legalistic rationing of God's grace, generations of ministers and lay preachers bear a heavy responsibility.

But the really vital faults of Dissenting communion services, as normally conducted, are nowadays more often faults of tone and atmosphere. A visiting Christian, who accepted the would-be-inclusive invitation to partake which is offered —not always after due thought—to 'all those who love the Lord Jesus', would often sense, I think, a widespread air of awkwardness, of spiritual squeamishness, forcing the congregation apart into individual private worlds when most of all they should be close to each other in closeness to the Lord. At bottom, this is probably a criticism of the whole quality of a church's life, but even our physical dispositions—scattered round the back pews—have something to do with it.

It is perhaps not wholly irrelevant to record that the most moving, and in a real sense the truest, communion service I have been privileged to share took place not in a church at all, but in someone's bed-sitting room, where twenty or thirty people sat in a circle and celebrated the Lord's Supper according to ancient Congregational practice, each delivering

[1] *Anglican-Methodist Relations, Some Institutional Factors* (Darton, Longman and Todd, 1061), p. 154.

to his neighbour the common loaf and the common cup, and experiencing a sacramental unity which after ten years' experience of Free Church worship I have yet to recognize again. I do not think that any Anglican—had one been present—would have been offended by that service, strange though it would have been to him. It is not when we are faithful to our liturgical traditions that we give offence, but when we are faithless.

Reunion Questions

I am acutely aware that much deeper exploration of all these and other questions is needed before the Free Churches, at all levels right down to 'each place', can advance beyond polite fencing with other denominations to the next stage of ecumenical encounter. But there are also grave organizational and sociological considerations affecting the search for unity in Britain, and it is at these I now glance.

In British church relations since the first world war, there is one important distinction of kind to be drawn, and that is the distinction between the ecumenical movement proper and the congruence of English Nonconformity in the Free Church Federal Council. The ecumenical movement is by definition a conversation between Christians of all traditions in all countries: Roman Catholics in Germany, Greek Orthodox in Armenia, Pentecostalists in South America, Anglicans in Japan. All may take part who will and, indeed, virtually all Christian traditions do take part, although the Roman Catholic participation is limited as yet to a few qualified theologians in the West, and there is a strong group of fundamentalist Protestants in the United States (mostly Baptists) who tend to regard the World Council of Churches, and nearly everyone else, as Communist-inspired. The English Free Churches—all honour to them—have through their leaders and theologians been deeply involved in this movement, and especially in its most spectacular achievement, the united Church of South India.

But this achievement was gained by *ad hoc* committees drawn from the Anglican communion and from the missionary societies representing the different denominations in South India. The organization through which the British Free Churches express such corporateness as they now enjoy, the Free Church Federal Council, had nothing to do with South India. Not entirely through its own fault, the FCFC, especially at local level, has more and more taken on the aspect of a defensive alliance against Christians of the 'Catholic' traditions, and against the domestic secular critics of what the Council interprets as the Nonconformist way of life. Lately, it has increasingly been overshadowed by the formation of local councils of churches, and by the national body, the British Council of Churches. England is no longer the centre of the ecclesiastical world, any more than of the political (it looked different when the Council of Evangelical Free Churches was formed in 1896); and because British churchmen were busy building up a valued and highly developed complex of ecumenical relationships with the younger Churches abroad, the search for organic reunion in this country, dating roughly from the Lambeth Appeal of 1920, has used the same patterns. No one has wanted to see the Church of England representatives ranged along one side of a rectangular table, with the FCFC ranged along the other. Lately, it has been the individual denominations—Anglican and Methodist, Anglican and Presbyterian, Congregational and Presbyterian—which have argued it out with each other at (so to speak) round tables.

In short, events have passed the Free Church Federal Council by, in a manner which looked unlikely when the Baptist J. H. Shakespeare made his moving appeal for Free Church Union at the annual meeting of the Council of Evangelical Free Churches in 1916. That council's successor, the FCFC, useful as it is as a focal point for recognition of the Free Churches on State occasions, has tended to become a cave of Adullam for people who are unable to find an outlet in their own denominations. Even in the field of education, where it has in the past done valuable work as a negotiating and occasionally a researching body, one can now envisage a time when the Council's functions could well be handed over entire to the British Council of Churches.

However, it is the failure of the Free Churches over the past fifty years to achieve anything more than the loosest possible federation among themselves which is more serious than the actual character of the federal body. True, it has been possible to ascribe this failure to the theological mistake, common among Free Churchmen of the past generation, of regarding the unity of all Christians as a vague 'spiritual' concept, quite without relevance for the actual constitution of the Body of Christ here on earth. But for all that, even the failure may have been providential. There is reason to believe that if the Free Churches had possessed the grace to achieve union in Britain forty years ago the effects would have been salutary but not ultimately satisfying; and that if Free Church Union took place now, it would be a nine days wonder but a long term disaster. It is clear from the frigid report on this subject recently published by the member bodies of the FCFC that this view now commands wide agreement in the Free Churches.[1]

A few of the reasons why this is so are relevant to the general thesis of this book. First, the result of such a union might in the long run be seriously divisive. It would further codify and institutionalize the major religious split in English life: that theological, social and cultural abyss which separates the Church of England from the rest. While the Free Churches remain separate, not only from the Established Church but from each other as well, they are somewhat less tempted to regard Anglicans as different cattle altogether, and

[1] However, for a contemporary statement of Nonconformist solidarity, see Healey, *Rooted in Faith* (Independent Press), published for the 1662 tercentenary.

they find it easier to remember ruefully how the shape of a
denomination's separateness has been determined by human
mistakes, and historical pressures on individual churchmen
at particular times. The creation of a 'Free Church of England'
could only obscure these humanizing oddities, and sever the
ropes which at present criss-cross over the great divide. The
new communion would be a monstrous monolith without
genuine roots and with a profoundly impoverished liturgy.
Its posture towards the Church of England could only be that
of its lowest common denominator. Its leaders would not
dare to be bolder than this l.c.d., for fear of the union over
which they presided breaking up again in mutual recrimina-
tion.

Secondly, it is a mistake to attribute homogeneity to, or
seek it for, the Free Churches. They are obviously natural
allies; though the alliances they drew up many years ago have
tended to outlast the social situations to which they were
addressed. But the Free Churches are not natural bed-fellows.
They are sufficiently different to irritate each other, but not
sufficiently different to supply each other's deficiencies. For
example, Congregationalists patently value intellectual and
aesthetic dignity rather more than Methodists do, and are
correspondingly short on evangelical zeal. It used to be said,
with some sociological accuracy, that Methodism or the Salvation Army converted one generation of a family, that Congregationalism educated the next, and that the third generation was received into the Church of England at a High level.
But although at the personal level Congregationalists and
Methodists, like Christians of all traditions, can learn from
each other, at the institutional level it is hard to visualize
what they could exchange.

It is far otherwise with Methodists and Anglicans. Methodists are not Dissenters by history, and many of them are not
Dissenters by conviction: they are displaced Anglican 'en-
thusiasts', with a love-hate relationship to the Church which
so unwisely, if at the time understandably, let them go.

Methodism is complementary to the Church of England because the dividing factor is not doctrine nor even (except in
relation to the status of ministers and to pastoral organization) church order, but social composition and attitude. Thus,
the healing of this particular division would contribute, not
only to the healing of schism in the Church, but to the healing of wider fissures in English society. A united Anglican-
Methodist Church would not dominate English culture in the
second half of the twentieth century. Both parties are now
much too bourgeois to be able to do that. But they would be a
little further in from the margin of life than any single communion is able to be today, and would precipitate a general
crack-up of the ecclesiastical iceberg as no other comparable
event could. Certainly, the union should only be a temporary
step on the way to a wider reunion, and it would in any case
confront great difficulties. Rural Methodism, especially, is in
such a parlous state that it would be in some danger of sink-
ing without trace, nor are the majority of Anglican country
vicars readily capable of handling such a situation with the
tact it would demand. A further and perhaps more serious
complication is that the Methodists, having at last almost
screwed up their courage to the point of admitting women
to the ministry, are now perceptibly drawing back for fear
of offending the Anglicans, on whom—with rare if distinguished exceptions—this light has not yet dawned. But this
is one of the problems which might well solve itself in the
new climate created by organic union.

Thirdly, it is highly unlikely that a united Free Church
would be able to persuade its constituent members to carry
their unity to the point where it hurt—the point where
ministerial distribution is rationalized and hundreds of
churches are shut. The Methodists by themselves have made
slow enough progress in this direction since Methodist Union,
thirty years ago. It was the establishment of the Church of
South India, not the union of Presbyterian and Congregational missions which preceded it, which had the truly re-

formative effect, largely because union involving the Anglicans compelled a much more radical examination of the nature of the Church. Even in terms of personalities, it is improbable that the men most likely to be acceptable as the leaders of a United Free Church would be the men best equipped to scrap our futile round of churchly organizations and nineteenth century ideas of mission, which might well survive a Free Church merger virtually undamaged.

This does not mean that all reunions of individual Free Church denominations with each other are to be excluded: far from it. Manning (who himself favoured a union of all the non-episcopal communions) anticipated thirty years ago that the Anglicans would 'sooner or later offer very favourable terms to the Methodists' and reach an *entente* with the Church of Scotland. He himself viewed this prospect with distaste, on the grounds that it would leave only the Congregationalists and the Baptists 'contending for St Paul's faith that grace comes freely from God, not legally by circumcision or episcopal ordination and confirmation'. He consequently argued very strongly for the union of Congregationalists and Presbyterians. We may look askance at his reasons, for episcopacy, as I have tried to argue, does not look quite the same thing today as it did in 1933. But we may agree wholeheartedly with his conclusion. It is really inexcusable that this particular union has not long since taken place. It nearly took place some 250 years ago. As Manning remarked, many Presbyterian practices in the conduct of public worship and the organization of the local church are Congregational practices which were only forgotten in the slovenly days of the last century. Nor, in the light of changes proposed, can one say that Congregationalism in Britain is decentralized while Presbyterianism is not: the difference is of degree. Never, in fact, has continued disunity been founded on so little apart from ignorance and inertia. And up to a point, Manning was right in his apprehensions about the future. When the bitterness generated by the 'Bishops' Report' has blown away and the Church of England *does* come to an *entente* with the Church of Scotland, Congregationalists will have much cause to bless the day that they made common cause with the English branch of the Kirk, and Presbyterians will have the gratification of knowing that they have become a 'bridge church' between the communion of Hooker and Whitgift and Laud, and the communion of Browne and Penry and Cromwell.[1] But woe unto both if they allow 'the appointed time' to slip by once again !

Three Possible Futures

It is time to sum up. It has been the general thesis of this book, and of this chapter in particular, that the decline of the Free Churches has gone very far—too far to be retrievable, as far as human calculation goes, unless fairly radical changes of direction are made soon. These changes include a much more determined concentration on various forms of reunion. But most important is for those outside the Free Churches to realize that decline, unless carried quite improbably to the point of total extinction, itself solves nothing. It merely makes an organization intractable. The change which the possible ossification of the Free Churches introduces into British church relations is the introduction of a time factor, a date by which some visible advance towards unity will have to be made if it is not to be too late. Anglicans here do well to be patient, and to realize how heavily the future of the English Church depends on lively, organically viable, confessionally alert Free Church denominations re-seeding themselves in this country over the next generation in preparation for reunion.

Three alternative versions of the future may be briefly sketched. The *first* can be instantly identified as fatal. This

---

[1] In fact, at the time of writing, the Church of Scotland and the Congregational churches there appear to be looking at the possibility of union with rather more sense of urgency than their English counterparts.

would be *the indefinitely prolonged independent existence of a rump Nonconformity.* It would be a religious society nostalgic for its nineteenth century homeland, but deprived of the leadership and driving force which alone could make this even faintly attainable. This possibility cannot be wholly discounted. Although the mass migrations out of the churches seem to be over, the social and theological revolutions which caused them could still recur in different forms, and the Free Churches show precious few signs as yet of learning to capitalize on their real assets, of attending to the rapidly-changing patterns of a society which conspicuously needs the qualities—responsibility, sound learning, a sense of direction, a sharp assessment of what is new under the sun—which the Puritan tradition provides. This task cannot be separated from Dissent's basic evangelistic obligation. And if the opportunity is missed, the Free Churches will remain stagnant, bereft of their young people as higher education reaches further and further down the social scale, too sore about their losses to see that they must cut their losses, and lacking the dynamism to go back to the source —the Bible— to reshape their church life.

In such an eventuality, the Church of England would gain by the influx of those whom the Free Churches lost. But many would have vanished from the fold altogether, and the prospect for any valuable Christian unity in Britain would be dim indeed. The robbed chapels would be bitter, and the proselytes would display the usual half-guilty intolerance of those who forsake the culture of their fathers. Sociologically, moreover, the results of such a development are unpredictable, because (in Britain at least) scarcely precedented. The process by which sects or movements harden into recognized, socially comprehensive denominations has never been thrown into reverse by the departure of their natural leaders in pursuit of a wider institutional loyalty. But, already, there is a double drain on the Free Churches. They are loyally supplying 'ecumenical civil servants' to run the emergent institutions of international and national Christendom. And they are losing young people (though the Methodists have several successes to their credit here). The Church of England too has her frustrated young people, but unlike their Free Church counterparts, they have nowhere else, other than secularism, which draws them away. In the end, if they remain Christian, most of them are compelled to work where God has called them. For Free Churchmen, the exit into other communions is too well signposted.

The *second* alternative before the Free Churches, of *premature reunion with Anglicanism*, is less distasteful, but still unsatisfactory. There are many signs that their intellectual and administrative leaders sincerely believe that unity, which they have with varying degrees of commitment accepted for the mission field, is ultimately the only hope for the home churches also. These denominational leaders are often the people most sharply aware of the merits possessed by their own particular form of churchmanship. They are also emotionally involved in the continued existence of their denominations as autonomous bureaucratic machines. But some have risen above these considerations. All that is in doubt is their ability to take the rest of their people with them, for the people are divided into those who know too little, and those who know (or rather feel) too much. If the ecumenically inclined leaders of the Free Churches contrived to take their denominations into reunion schemes without at least a significant proportion of the rank and file first becoming alive to their own heritage and aware of the sacrifices demanded by ecumenical encounter, disaster would ensue. Those shreds of Dissenting vitality which—for instance—were just about enough to prevent the British Council of Churches in its early days from reflecting *too* accurately the social and political attitudes of Lord Fisher, would be blown away from the British ecclesiastical scene. The Church in England would become a huge bureaucratic juggernaut, managed by the uninspired for the uninformed. Reunion, it may be hazarded, is not the will of God until it is willed by, rather than wished on, 'each place'.

And even if the peril of the don't-want-to-knows could be averted, there would remain the peril of the atavists. This is a problem which is rarely treated with seriousness and precision. However, Bishop Stephen Neill has recently done so.

> Scarcely any union will come into being without leaving behind a faithful little Zion, a caucus or a rump; naturally the choice of terms will vary with the convictions of those who use them. . . . Nothing in the world is so hard as for a majority to decide at what point it will enter into union with other Christians against the wishes of a minority of its own members. How small a minority should be allowed to hold up plans to which the vast majority of a Church has agreed? No clear answer can be given. Yet it may be thought that the great majorities of 90 per cent and more (found in Scotland in 1928 and South India in 1947) were right in moving forward.

But sometimes there are far larger minorities. A third of the Presbyterian Church refused to enter the United Church of Canada in 1925.

> The strain on wills and nerves and consciences, penetrating into the heart of united families and dividing them, was so terrible that there are those who even after the lapse of thirty-five years prefer not to speak of all that they suffered in those days.[1]

I do not answer this question : I merely pose it. But it is idle to suppose that in Britain, of all countries, a united Church could ever be accepted unanimously, and equally idle, I think, to suppose that any individual reunion scheme should be entered into here with a third of the people for whom it was intended staying out. There are also, of course, immensely complex legal and financial issues involved in al-

[1] *Twentieth Century Christianity* (Collins, 1961), pp. 343-4.

most any major reunion scheme likely to be contemplated in Britain.

However, the sooner cool discussion of these and other issues begins, the sooner we shall convince ourselves and others that the ecumenical movement in Britain is serious, permanent and determined. Here lies my *third* alternative: *reunion in good time.* The status quo in British church relations cannot last for ever, and it will be astonishing and catastrophic if it lasts beyond the end of the century. If the rising generation in the Free Churches begins to feel that no significant change can be expected in its lifetime, we expose ourselves to a new stampede out of the chapels, no less injurious than the one which has already occurred. There is no future for the Free Churches as they are, short of reunion. Patterns and timetables are a more doubtful matter. John Lawrence, who asserts that we ought to be able to attain full visible unity within the next ten or twenty years between Anglicans, Presbyterians, Congregationalists, Methodists, many Baptists, the Society of Friends and the Salvation Army, seems to me wildly optimistic. But I would personally hope to see no less than a Church of England visibly united with the Methodists, in full communion with the Church of Scotland, and moving by this means towards visible organic union with what would by then be the other mainstream English confession, a union of Congregationalists, Presbyterians and Baptists.[1] If we want a watchword for our time— and the Free Churches have always been fond of watchwords —we might do worse than re-write Robert Browne and plead for 'reunion without tarying for anie', conscious that reunion worth the name would itself lead to a degree of Reformation which goes beyond anything that we are able to

---

[1] The prospects for reunion schemes involving Baptists have been greatly helped by experience in the negotiations for the United Church of North India, in which they have been included.

imagine at present. We may not tarry for any, because the Holy Spirit does not tarry for us.

Even so, there is a time of waiting to be tackled. Most people seriously concerned with reunion are now convinced that the weight of endeavour in the next few years must be thrown on the local church. Scotland and the affair of the Bishops' Report are largely responsible for this. It is true that in communities where at least a proportion of the local Anglican and Free Churches are 'coming alive', and are aware of the wide-open opportunities for doing new things together, the laity have been given not just the patience to hang on for another decade or two, but a sense of profoundly changing attitudes. The local variations in inter-church relationships—even over a distance of a mile or two between one Gloucestershire village and another, one Liverpool suburb and another—are most striking. Yet even through the national and regional machinery of Dissenting denominations, something can be done. Systems of church order which, as I suggested earlier, are highly vulnerable to wrecking parties may also prove open to single-minded reforming parties as well. And when all is said, the Free Churches do have certain advantages in the task which lies before them. They are generally free at local level to explore new ways out of the prison in which they are lodged, with no one to say to them nay but themselves. They can still recover their identity quite quickly (one has seen it done in particular churches inside two or three years, given a minister of genius). They are also free at national level to express their characteristic graces in whatever ecclesiastical pattern is found agreeable to the Word of God and the needs of the time. But as things are, they will have to work for their freedom.

INDEX